Minicourses

In the past few years, the minicourse has emerged as a way of presenting subject content that appeals to students, teachers, and administrators alike. For students the minicourse can be a highly motivating form, encouraging in-depth learning in content areas they would otherwise be able only to survey. Teachers find particular rewards in presenting detailed content on subjects in which they have particular interest and expertise. In addition, they find that fewer learning and discipline problems are present when students are involved in these courses. Administrators, too, respond affirmatively to the ideal combination of flexibility and structure minicourses provide in their schools.

This report in the *Developments in Classroom Instruction* series offers a realistic discussion of the minicourse movement, as well as practical step-by-step guidance for teachers in the planning and implementation of minicourse curricula. Two minicourse models—one on America's Maritime Heritage and one on Sports Literature—give teachers complete resource lists, as well as detailed instructions for setting up minicourses in their classrooms. In discussing the planning and structuring of minicourses, Dr. Wm. Ray Heitzmann, as member of the education faculty of Villanova University, shows teachers how to develop course objectives, organize students in various groupings, allocate time and space, balance observation and study activities, and evaluate the effectiveness of the course. He also shows how minicourses can be developed for interdisciplinary studies. He discusses the use of print and non-print media and provides a selected bibliography of readings on the minicourse, as well as lists of minicourses offered by schools in various parts of the United States.

Dr. Heitzmann is the author of numerous articles on social studies teaching and other areas of education. His publications include *Educational Games and Simulations* in NEA's *What Research Says to the Teacher* series.

MINICOURSES

Minicourses

by Wm. Ray Heitzmann

National Education Association
Washington, D.C.

Acknowledgments

The manuscript has been reviewed by Helen M. Edmonston, retired social studies teacher, Montgomery County (Maryland) Public Schools.

NEA gratefully acknowledges the permissions given to use the following:

"Appendix A: Successful Free Forming Checklist for Schools." *Nation's Schools*, Volume 90, Number 1, July 1972. Copyright © 1972 by McGraw-Hill, Inc. Reprinted with permission.

"Chart 1." *Teaching and Media: A Systematic Approach* by Vernon S. Gerlach and Donald P. Ely. Copyright © 1971 by Prentice-Hall, Inc. Adapted by permission of Prentice-Hall, Inc., Englewood Cliffs, New Jersey.

Library of Congress Cataloging in Publication Data

Heitzmann, William Ray.
  Minicourses.

  (Developments in classroom instruction)
  Bibliography: p.
  1. Curriculum planning.   I. Title.   II. Series.
LB1570. H435   375'.001   76-39939
ISBN 0-8106-1806-0
ISBN 0-8106-1805-2 pbk.

CONTENTS

Introduction

The minicourse, a relatively recent curriculum development, has received favorable reactions from students, teachers, and administrators. It has been well received by students because it answers the need for relevancy and, consequently, can be a highly interesting and motivational area of the curriculum. Teachers like the minicourse for much the same reasons, seeing it turning students on and additionally providing an opportunity to teach a course of special interest. Unfortunately, in the traditional school setting a teacher can rarely spend much time on a particular area that might be his or her specialty. But a social studies teacher can now offer minicourses in a specific field, such as "The Presidency" or "Social Psychology"; similarly, the English teacher can have courses such as "Filmmaking" or "Creative Writing." The range of minicourse offerings seems unlimited; in some cases, co-curricular activities become part of the minicourse curriculum. After-school activities such as photography, bachelor homemaking, and self-defense have become part of the regular program in some schools.

School administrators like the flexibility that the minicourse can offer because it provides a progressive yet structured curriculum. While there may be concern about the extra paper work and the initial adjustment problem, these are really relatively minor difficulties, and the benefits are certainly worth the investment in time.

It should be pointed out, however, that not all is rosy with the minicourse movement. Recent studies showing high school graduates deficient in basic skills—writing, reading, speaking, citizenship, listening, critical thinking and others, as well as knowledge of our nation's heritage—have provided ammunition for those critical of progressive curricula. Nothing can destroy a good idea quicker than improper planning prior to implementation. Perhaps in no other area of the school scene is this maxim truer than in curriculum innovation. Obviously, minicourse programs could do nothing inherently to oppose or discourage the development of basic process skills. In fact, mini's can be offered specifically for the purpose of skill improvement.

This report offers the classroom teacher a procedure to develop a minicourse that will be justifiable to the administrator and school board member as well as to the community and that will, above all, become a learning experience for students.

1. What Are Minicourses?

Minicourses can generally be characterized as short-term, academic or nonacademic, high interest, in-depth instructional courses. The grass roots nature of the minicourse movement partially accounts for the varied form minicourses have taken. Since it is neither the outgrowth of an educational theory nor the result of a dictate from a state education department nor the findings from a federal research grant, the minicourse is uniquely adaptable to the particular needs of a school or student body.

The time and timing of minicourse programs varies greatly. Following are some of the formats provided by schools:

1. A two-week end-of-the-year program organized and conducted by the senior class.
2. Four ten-week units in which the student would take at least one course during each segment from a grouping of courses.
3. A series of forty, nine-week courses in history and the social sciences for students in grades ten through twelve.
4. An offering of 350 courses for all students, presented during one week while the traditional school program is suspended.
5. Courses in English and social studies offered for one or two weeks.
6. A three-day minicourse marathon.
7. A one-day program where mini's are offered for extended class periods.

Some schools offer a minicourse program in place of study halls and during lunch periods. Others provide a smorgasbord from which students select four nine- or ten-week or six six-week courses to satisfy the English or social studies graduation requirement. Still others offer minicourses as electives over and above the regular requirements, entirely for enrichment.

Characterized by student and teacher input and design, and dedicated to the idea of structured alternatives, the minicourse bandwagon appears on the education scene, offering the promise to administrators and school boards of low cost innovation and the promise to students of curriculum and instructional reform, which in some cases takes the form of no tests, no grades, and no homework. Typically, these courses with their action orientation have stimulated bored students and static teachers, bringing them closer together in a way that education was intended to do.

The difficulty in generalizing about minicourses may provide some answer to their success. During the 1960's curriculum projects characterized curriculum development, but the project developers were disappointed by the lack of adoption. Part of the reason was the rigidity (often teacher-proof) and consequent difficulty in adaptation to local circumstances. Minicourses fortunately have not had such a fate, experiencing only mild criticism in a few, rare cases. Proper planning and organization can serve not only to silence such criticism but to improve the entire personnel and public relations situation.

2. Why Minicourses?

Every school program must have a rationale for its existence, particularly when ever-tightening school budgets require school personnel to justify each expenditure.

Some of the reasons for establishing minicourses are found in the answers to the following questions posed by Albert Oliver, *Curriculum Improvement, A Guide to Problems, Principles and Procedures:*[1]

1. How many dropouts occur in the school?
2. Are there many discipline and other student personnel problems?
3. Are the high school graduates successful in college as undergraduates?
4. Are the graduates placed in the community's industries, businesses, and professions?
5. How well do the pupils do on standardized tests?
6. How adequate are the records on individual pupils? What provisions are made to have them available to students?
7. How effective is the guidance program?
8. What seems to be the school's morale?
9. What is the percentage of failures?
10. What provision is made for individual differences and interests?

Obviously, some of the above questions are more pertinent than others; however, those that appear less important should not be discarded or overlooked. For example, if the answer to question 7 shows a serious need for improvement of the guidance program, might not a minicourse partially solve the problem—perhaps, "How to Obtain Your First Job" or "How to Do Well on the College Boards"?

Affective Education

Beginning in the late 1960's and continuing almost unabated to the present, authors such as Charles E. Silberman, James Herndon, William Glasser, John Holt, Paul Goodman, and Dorothy Rogers have written that schools contained psychological environments which were not conducive to promoting learning, largely because they failed in the affective domain. Students, subjected to repressive and nonresponsive teachers and administrators, reacted by dropping out either physically or mentally. This literature, calling for radical school reform, coincided with student unrest and protest and provided some documentation for critique of schools. It is not surprising, therefore, to learn that the first minicourses made their appearance in the late 1960's.

One example of such a development has been recorded by two researchers, Arthur D. Roberts and Robert K. Gable:

> In the spring of 1969, the students of Walt Whitman High School in Bethesda, Maryland, ran a one-week experiment in free form education during which there were no required classes, no grades and traditional class groupings. A list of 242 subjects was drawn up and 150 guest lecturers, including many of Whitman's most talented students, were asked to participate. Whitman students were then asked to sign up for the subjects they wished to study; these ranged from European archeology to science fiction. Many of the courses were action oriented. Students interned at local and regional planning offices, worked at newspapers, stores, or served as student aides in classes for the handicapped, helped U.S. Senators with their mail and so forth.
>
> It was from this experiment and similar variations on the theme that the minicourse movement was born.[2]

The desire that students leave school liking to learn at least as much as when they entered was what initiated the movement. This is certainly a noble goal. However, in some cases this desire for a positive affective experience resulted in courses that were nothing more than exotic-sounding titles. That is, course content tended to be shallow, objectives for the organization of instruction were not written, instructional materials (media and materials) that were frequently difficult to obtain were not used, and planning for time and space utilization was inadequate. Consequently, failure and disappointment were experienced by teachers and students, supplying critics of school reform with examples of school mismanagement and poor teaching. Despite these failures, the desire to humanize the learning process continues to rank as one of main trends in school reform. Conference speakers, journal and book authors, workshop directors, and educational theorists daily extol educators to humanize their schools. Minicourses are an efficient means to do this.

Some of Oliver's questions listed earlier in this chapter measure the schools' performance in the affective domain (e.g., school morale, dropout percentage). Answers to these questions may indicate that substantial improvements are needed, and minicourses can help enable these needed improvements as well as contribute to making an already good school even better.

Research Results

Research studies, although limited in number and somewhat lacking in total experimental control,[3] report that minicourses have achieved their desired results in the affective domain. Sylvester Kohut of Dickinson College studied a rural school district in central Pennsylvania. He found that students enrolled in a minicourse social studies curriculum showed a significant improvement in attitude toward both the teacher's performance and the social studies course, in comparison to students enrolled in a traditional program.[4] These results are supported by the similar findings of Donald Gudaitis, then coordinator of secondary education, Westfield, New Jersey (a suburban upper middle-class district).

Concerning student attitude change, he writes the following:

> The investigation showed that the majority of students did feel more positive toward the study of social studies. There were several indicators that tended to confirm their replies. Students stated they found the courses more interesting, stimulating and a number found learning easier. . . . Many students found classes less boring.[5]

Testimonials from faculty and students lend further verification to these empirical studies. Robert Hayward, an English teacher at

Hamilton-Wenham Regional High School, Hamilton, Massachusetts, said that "attendance was the best it had been all year."[6] Another English teacher at the same school announced, "This is the first time I've ever taught kids who wanted to be in my subject. It's wonderful!"[7] A student commented, "Being *allowed* to learn instead of being made to learn changes everyone's attitude. This is how all education should be structured."[8]

Affective Education—Summary

The growing trend for schools to operate in the domain of feelings, values, and attitudes coupled with an increased desire to humanize learning makes the adoption of the minicourse approach a prudent if not obvious strategy for school districts to implement. Furthermore, the increased wish by classroom teachers to operate in the affective domain makes the minicourse approach a natural. For example, many educators are presently attempting to design strategies that will result in a positive self-concept on the part of the learner. The use of student ideas as input in suggesting minicourses, in aiding course organization, and even in teaching part or all of a course can serve as a powerful technique in promoting self-esteem. Student involvement in planning and teaching appears quite widespread. Hayward states that "Teachers are more inclined than heretofore to enlist student help in planning units of study."[9] Of course, in this college type of arrangement, all students participate in the curriculum development process by voting for the courses they wish to take. Roberts and Gable suggest that students could "quite possibly teach a course themselves if they have a unique ability."[10] Likewise, the heterogeneous grouping of these courses serves to remove the social stigma frequently attached to those in the remedial, lower or nonacademic sections or tracks—an important consideration if one wishes to encourage self-worth.

The effect upon teachers should not be overlooked. Teacher morale has improved for several reasons: they have the opportunity to share a particular academic specialty (e.g., sports writing) or nonacademic interest (e.g., gardening) or to pursue along with students an area of curiosity (e.g., spiritualism and the occult). These courses, therefore, appeal both on an intellectual (professional) level and on a personal level. Teachers frequently get to know students better than in conventional curricular arrangements. As a result, the humanity of teachers and teaching becomes plainly visible.

14

Cognitive and Psychomotor Education

The major justification for the minicourse arrangement has been its affective advantages; however, its value in terms of the acquisition of knowledge also needs examination, particularly as there have been serious shortcomings in the cognitive dimension.

This alternative curricular arrangement offers the opportunity for the study of a specific subject in greater depth than is permitted in the normal traditional arrangement. However, this can be a two-edged sword—providing an interesting smorgasbord of in-depth courses on one hand and a fragmented nonsequential arrangement (in some schools) on the other hand. This latter problem has results in a situation where the learner never obtains a feel for a body of knowledge because of serious knowledge gaps.

In some schools, the one-unit requirement for social studies can be satisfied by the selection of any nine (six, twelve) four-week minicourses from a list of thirty. It is possible to choose minicourses in such a way that students upon graduation will be unfamiliar with many areas of history and the social science. For example, recent studies show a serious lack of knowledge of American history among some high school graduates that is the result of this smorgasbord approach.

To ensure that students are exposed to important subjects, teachers could act as advisors, helping to guide selection. Schools could require a basic foundation course as a prerequisite or require that students select their courses from a series of groupings thus assuring a more balanced education. These above arrangements can be the best of both possible worlds: they can provide alternatives for students yet guarantee them cognitive growth. Students need to have a basic understanding of the bodies of knowledge and to be armed with basic process skills in order to face life successfully and to achieve self-actualization. [11]

There are other arguments for the cognitive justification of a minicourse curriculum. For gifted students these courses offer enrichment opportunities that challenge them by offering the opportunity for sophisticated study. Slower students already permitted to sign up for more academic courses can likewise respond to this new challenge: "We were amazed by their sophisticated handling of difficult subjects in mixed discussion groups." Robert Hayward further commented, "They sometimes outdid the brightest seniors in their penetrating observations about Bergman's *The Virgin Spring* or *Smiles of a Summer Night*." [12] For the nonmotivated, apathetic, chronic-problem, frequent-failure student, the minicourse may be the salvation. The students' high interest that comes from freedom of choice, having an alternative, provides the spark for these students. Additionally, if these students do fail or receive a low grade, they can recover with a new teacher and a different course. Those with short attention spans, often a trademark of slower students, continually gain fresh starts as they move through the sequence. Such a program offers an opportunity to all students, but perhaps its real value lies in the rare chance it offers to the broad spectrum of exceptional children for learning successes.

Rarely do the so-called academic courses provide opportunities for psychomotor development. This is generally left to the specialists—physical education, vocational and technical education, art, home economics, and business education. The action orientation of many minicourses finds students engaged in out-of-school activities—for example, conducting oral history interviews, collecting water samples, filmmaking, performing service tasks for senior citizens or institutionalized persons, videotaping meetings of committees (town or city council, court proceedings, school board meetings), and practicing scuba diving. The program also opens the door for the college-bound student, traditionally restricted to a tight curriculum, to investigate and develop survival skills. For example: "Automotive and Cycle Repair," "Making Leisure Count," "You Are What You Eat," "The Law and You," "Baking and Cooking."[13]

Those departments concerned with developing psychomotor skills would undoubtedly offer a series of in-depth minicourses designed especially for the students majoring in that department. These minicourses should be both challenging and educational.

Rarely does an innovation in education offer the opportunity to develop the learner's capacity in all three spheres of human endeavor—cognitive, affective, and psychomotor. For this reason, minicourses deserve the serious consideration of teachers wishing to provide alternatives within a structured yet flexible setting.

3. Systematic Development

Need for Planning

While the need for planning is important in an endeavor, academic or not, it is a prerequisite for developing a successful mini-course. For example, Arthur Roberts and Robert Gable warn, "Teachers may try to compress too much into a mini. The result could well be an extensive tobacco auction."[1] Robert Hayward further emphasizes this need:

> At first look, minicourses seemed a simple experiment to run: for two weeks merely stop all classes that consist only of seniors and have the seniors reschedule themselves into special minicourses. But this was easier said than done . . . between preparing and teaching all-new material, using every extra period in the day, and living through the excitement of those two weeks, most of us teachers were exhausted.[2]

Despite the above testimonials, some authors unfortunately have misguided teachers. Adele H. Stern, Chairperson of the English Department at Montclair High School, New Jersey, suggests, "All such a program requires is enthusiasm."[3] Allan A. Glatthorn, University of Pennsylvania and former principal of the Abington High School, Pennsylvania, gives the following guidance: "There is no need for elaborate planning or systematic analysis."[4] We might well ask ourselves if the real weakness in the development of the minicourse is not the dilettante approach that forsakes serious development for superficial planning. The mini program holds out such promise for success that it should not be jeopardized by a sloppy, callous, or less than well thought-out approach. In this day of accountability teachers cannot afford the luxury of less than adequate preplanning.

William G. Swenson, Chairperson of the Department of English at the John F. Kennedy High School, New York, states that ". . . ideally the minicourse electives program should have a full year for planning, development, and supplying before the actual program begins."[5] Realistically such preparation prior to program commencement is rarely possible because of the spontaneous nature of the mini and the desire by everyone involved to begin. Therefore careful time utilization must be arranged to maximize course organization and, hopefully, its consequent success. This may seem an overstatement of one's position; however, the evidence for this approach is repeatedly offered by experienced minicourse designers. "Schoolmen say students love it but they also warn that without proper planning, free forming (minicourses) can be a fiasco . . . plan ahead sounds like standard advice, but it means way ahead when you're talking about free forming."[6]

Chart 1 provides a guideline for use by teachers that can serve as a tool to systematic minicourse development. The emphasis in using this chart and other guidelines is to aid the classroom teacher as opposed to providing extensive advice for the school's curriculum committee or the administrator's role. (Appendix A provides suggestions for the school's approach.)

Input

Teachers, designers, administrators, and evaluators agree that a minicourse program "is an effective way to get teacher and student input into the curriculum."[7] Recent educational administrative theorists have encouraged school districts to provide mechanisms for community input into the school programs. However, many schools have yet to adopt such a scheme. For these schools, the mini approach can serve to move in this direction. Roberts and Gable argue for this approach: "Teacher-pupil cooperation is especially apropos if an affective outcome that we seek is a change in both student and teacher attitudes."[8] If affective learning is one of the goals that is articulated for the minicourse program, then a mechanism for community and student input should be provided.

CHART 1

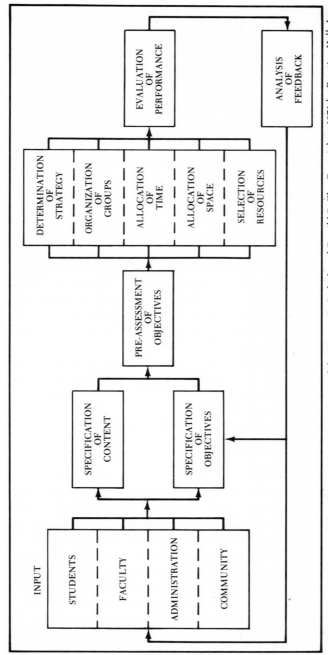

Adapted from *Teaching and the Media: A Systematic Approach* by Vernon S. Gerlach and Donald P. Ely. Copyright © 1971 by Prentice-Hall, Inc. Used with permission.

The researchers tell us that most schools do this. Daniel Parkinson in an Ohio study found that "Students play a role in course development in 74.8 percent of the schools."[9] Similarly, John Guenther and Robert Ridgeway discovered that "in the majority of schools, minicourses were developed with student input."[10] The benefits of such a strategy are obvious: "Favorable attitudes are frequently developed when a group of people are involved in decision-making."[11] Surely part of the success of mini's must be attributed to the positive feeling that students receive as part of initial participation in developing the offerings.

If the school has an established community council or school curriculum committee, then it will obviously be used in the early developing stages. This group may be the motivating force for the program. In addition, the group may suggest some courses, such as, "How to Obtain a Job," "Polish-American Heritage," "Self-Defense for Women," "How to Study in College." The majority of the courses will originate from surveys of what interests students and teachers. For example, Gudaitis reporting on the social studies minicourse program at Westfield High School stated, "The entire junior class was surveyed about their concerns and interest in United States history."[12] In answering the requests for these courses, the teacher frequently faces the burden of difficult course planning. According to Roberts and Gable, a "possible disadvantage is the large number of preparations a teacher may be required to make during a session or school year."[13] This general problem was echoed by Parkinson: "Other problems cited by several faculty members include difficulties in fitting teacher strengths to student interests."[14] The reply to this situation is systematic planning and hard work in obtaining the requisite knowledge and teaching materials.[15]

Specification of Objectives

At this point in time most teachers have experiences in one form or another in the behavioral objectives movement. While this trend has somewhat subsided, teachers generally agree that behavioral objectives have educational value. First, they aid in the planning (outline, organizing, sequencing) of the student learning experiences. Second, they help teachers in the construction of measures of student evaluation. Third, they can help students find out what is expected of them. Fourth, they can be extremely useful in pre-assessment of students' competencies at the beginning of a course, particularly in a minicourse where there can be great heterogeneity of student experience and ability.

Robert Mager, author of *Preparing Instructional Objectives* and an early leader in the behavioral objectives approach to instruction, lists criteria for specific objectives:

  a. It should be stated in performance terms (explain the behavior of the learner at the termination of the lesson, unit, course).
  b. Give the conditions under which the behavior takes place.
  c. A statement of minimum acceptable level of performance.[16]

In preparing objectives and test questions, Benjamin Bloom (author of *Taxonomy of Educational Objectives: Cognitive Domain*) and David Krathwohl (author of *Taxonomy of Educational Objectives: Affective Domain*) provide excellent guides for writing higher level goals that permit and encourage the learner to operate within the higher levels of behavior. Psychomotor objectives have been found easier to write and assess, due to the direct observational nature of the domain.

This first stage will probably take longer to prepare than the others; however, once accomplished course construction and the remaining steps should easily be accomplished. With minicourses, teachers must be vigilant not to write objectives that are unattainable because they are too numerous or because the learning experiences used to reach the objective cannot be completed in the allotted time. Undoubtedly, there will be an affective emphasis in the objectives, as it's in this area of learning that minicourses carry their greatest impact. Also, many teachers will find themselves writing more psychomotor objectives than they have in traditional courses because of the action nature of the program (such as, community activities, arts and crafts, field trips).

The following are examples of objectives that might be used with the sample minicourses:

America's Maritime Heritage

  1. High Level Cognitive
     The student will give a speech analyzing the reasons for peoples' lack of concern with the nation's maritime tradition.
  2. Middle Level Affective
     The student will write a letter to his or her U.S. Representative that supports legislation for the improvement of the merchant marine, U.S. shipping, and the Navy.
  3. High Level Psychomotor
     The student will construct a model ship from a kit or with original materials, or the student will take a walking tour of a harbor or a tour of a decommissioned historic ship.

Sports Literature

1. Low Level Cognitive
   The student will be able to list the categories of sports literature with an example of one item (book, article) for each category.
2. High Level Affective
   The student will volunteer to give book talks on sports biographies to children at the local library on Saturday mornings in January and February.
3. High Level Psychomotor
   The student will demonstrate a drill (exercise) that will help a potential basketball player develop the ability to dribble with the left hand only, for two minutes while running. The drill can be from a sports technique book or developed originally.

The interdependent nature of instructional objectives, particularly for use with minicourses, can be observed from the above examples. Objectives developed in consort with content can serve to help teachers be more efficient in choosing minicourse content.

Specification of Content

The general content for the course will come from the title. It remains for the instructor to specify the appropriate emphasis. With the very brief minicourse (one to five days) teachers must be vigilant and try not to cover too much material. Students come to drink from the fountain of knowledge—teachers must not turn on a firehouse and drown them. Similarly, too much content can reduce the affective value of the course and curtail the spontaneity of the discussions and the interactions it entails. Teachers designated to instruct a mini in a given area of interest should be cautious not to fall into this trap. Because they know so much about this area and enjoy it so much, they assume students feel the same way.

The other side of the coin also presents difficulties—the assignment of a course with content unfamiliar or only partially familiar to the teacher. In these situations, there exist some avenues to fill in the knowledge gaps. The following are some practical sources:

1. Survey other schools ot obtain a copy of course outline, syllabus, objectives. (Colleges might be an unexpected source.)
2. Examine review books. They usually outline a subject area in a brief yet complete manner. In most situations a review book will not be available for the specific area of the course; however, one chapter of the review book may cover the topic of the mini. For example, a review book in psychology and biology will contain in-

formation for a course on human sexuality. Sometimes a review book will be available for an exact course, such as, "Social Psychology." Sometimes a quick trip to a college bookstore will result in obtaining the book and will get the course preparation off to a successful start.

3. Visit local bookstores and survey the shelves for appropriate paperbacks for teacher as well as student usage. Some authors believe, "The true mini-course/electives program is primarily a paperback program using a wide range of materials." Several of the paperback companies now provide materials directly for the education market. Bantam Books, Inc., offers course guides ("Science Fiction," "Futuristics," "Women's Studies") that can be especially helpful.

4. Talk with librarians for suggestions. One of the best, and frequently overlooked, sources are encyclopedias. Their up-to-date, well-organized, and nicely written articles constitute an excellent source of information, and many of these companies offer reprints that can be used by students. Librarians can also direct teachers to other resources, such as a vertical file.

5. Naturally, the teacher will wish to consult articles, books, textbooks, indices, in search for information. A trip to a large public or college library reference room to examine the publications and the handbooks of the professional societies can often provide leads to sources of content. Also, the subject guide to *Books in Print* can save time in locating potential materials.

6. If it's available, an information retrieval system, such as ERIC, may aid in locating course content.

The sample minicourses suggest two possible arrangements. First, when dealing with an unfamiliar topic, the division of it into units or lessons can provide a structure useful to teacher and student. Secondly, in shorter courses, it may be necessary first to familiarize the class with the various categories and, then, investigate one in depth. For example, "Introduction to Political Science," a two-day minicourse, may be arranged into some of the following divisions:

    I. Government
      a. Comparative
      b. American
      c. Municipal, State
   II. Political theory and philosophy
 III. Political behavior
 IV. International relations
  V. Law

Following a brief review of these, the instructor might say, "Be-cause of time constraints, we will only cover 'political be-havior'—discussing such items as voter turnout, ethnic voting, party participation, and campaign techniques." Or, "... we can only cover one of these five topics. Which would you prefer to study?" This latter position will call for additional preparation.

In organizing the content, the following ideas should be kept in mind:

1. Progress from concrete objects or experiences to more abstract ideas
2. Progress from simple to elementary to more complex manipula-tions, principles, or understandings
3. Progress from isolated facts to integrated principles or rela-tionships
4. Progress from specific to general, i.e., inductive
5. Progress from general to specific, i.e., deductive
6. Progress from unknown to known.
7. When teaching a process, progress from beginning to end, i.e., temporal or chronological ordering[17]

The specification of content and objectives in terms of a mini-course program permits the teacher to maximize effectiveness in planning and organizing. It also serves a second general purpose to provide for a pre-assessment of students.

Pre-Assessment of Objectives

Present thinking on pretesting or pre-evaluation is summarized by the following:

> Usually the student begins the module (minicourse) with some skills, information and/or competencies which are relevant to what he is supposed to learn. We usually refer to relevant competencies which the learner brings to the learning experience as the *entry be-havior* of the learner. Since it would be a waste of time and effort to "teach" competencies that the learner already possesses, it is the job of the instructional developer (teacher) to determine what related ca-pabilities the student has already acquired.[18]

This concept has special applicability to most minicourse ar-rangements; however, probably because of time, it should not be used in the one-day mini arrangement. The abilities and experiences of the learner vary greatly on entry to the minicourse. The instruc-tor, on the basis of preassessment, can do two things. The first thing would be to identify the student who can make direct contributions to the course in terms of a presentation or demonstration. For example, in "Baking Skills for Young Men" there might be some appropriate comments from a class member about some items (apple turnover) or techniques (dough preparation) he has mastered. Peer presentations provide opportunities for growth for both the audience and the demonstrator. Additionally, it enables the teacher to act in an efficient manner by maximizing the resources available to him/her. The second thing that the instructor could do would be to identify the students' competencies so that the teacher can emphasize or de-emphasize certain areas of the content accordingly. Also, students doing well can be released for different learning experiences in independent study. All learners will have a good idea of what the course will require. The diverse background of the learner coming into the mini frequently necessitates individualizing instruction. Undoubtedly, this partially accounts for the research finding that "over 40 percent use contracts, packets or Unipacks."[19]

Pre-assessment exists as an important step in any systematic approach to instruction. With most minicourse approaches it can serve the teacher as a useful tool for identifying students' differences and designing their learning experiences accordingly. It should also be mentioned that in some situations students will need to be counseled to withdraw from certain minicourses on the basis of prior performance.

Determination of Strategy

Strategy in this context is the broad or generic use as opposed to specific teaching methods. The following is a list of these widely used strategies:

    a. Discovery (inquiry)
    b. Expository
    c. Group (simulations, learning games)
    d. Individualized (programmed instruction, packets)
    e. Field based (community based)
    f. Demonstration (practice)
    g. Basic skills

a) Discovery (Inquiry)

Discovery learning presently enjoys popularity among educators; some believe this should be the basis of all instruction in schools. At this point in time, the consensus of researchers is in support of this strategy. However, because of its emphasis on critical thinking, problem solving, and involvement, most educators feel it should be part of the repertoire of each teacher. Because of time constraints placed on them and their desire to cover content areas, many teachers have withheld total teaching commitment, preferring to use it in combination with expository teaching.

The actual use of this strategy takes several forms. Some teachers use it in asking classroom questions, preferring to draw out answers. Others construct packets of materials from which students draw generalizations and some use commercially prepared kits. The explosion of knowledge in recent years has provided impetus for this teaching strategy, as classroom teachers realize they can no longer cover everything. For Plato it is the habit ("form") of mind and not its contents ("substance") that is under greater scrutiny. Educators, similarly, should consider inquiry learning for their mini's.

b) Expository

The teacher as information giver is the basic premise of expository teaching. The teaching method associated with this strategy is generally lecturing, although it may take the form of reading materials and viewing films. Because of the brevity of some mini's, lecturing might be used more than the teachers or students wish. The value of this technique is its use in covering large amounts of information in a short period of time. Undoubtedly, this accounts for its endurance over time. One of the assumptions of this method, that the teacher (and books) is a repository of knowledge, surely has a basis in truth. Another argument for this approach rests in the fact that there exist certain times in every course when a large amount of information must be presented. Frequently, a well-planned and well-illustrated lecture is the best way to reach the instructional objective that has a strong content (product) basis.

Many teachers already combine this strategy with others in their teaching and wisely vary method according to objective. Minicourse teachers must be vigilant not to permit themselves to fall into the lecture trap, thereby undermining the action orientation of minicourses and stifling the enthusiasm connected with them.

c) Group

Group learning as a teaching strategy has long been a technique used by educators and has taken the form of group projects, teams, and group oral reports. Recently, a bandwagon effect has taken place as educators and students have engaged in educational simulations and learning games at every grade level and in every subject area. These simulation games have been shown not only to be of great interest and highly motivating for students, but also to promote cognitive and affective learnings. Consider the following summary of the research evidence:

> Students' enjoyment of simulations seems to be related to their need for active rather than passive involvement . . . simulations permit students to utilize their natural tendencies—walking, talking, and they often require group involvement and healthy competition. Finally, they offer a respite from the more routine classroom procedures.

And more importantly:

> Several studies have concluded that students taught through educational games and simulations learn more content than do students taught in a conventional manner . . . the majority of research studies reveal that involvement in learning games and simulations can indeed change the attitude of participants.[20]

This valuable and flexible strategy can serve to achieve minicourse objectives or even form the basis for an entire course, such as, "Learning from Games" or "A Simulation Games Approach to Twentieth Century American History."

d) Individualized

One of the curious phenomena presently taking place in curriculum and instructional innovation is the trend toward individualized learning and its opposite of group learning. For years, educational psychologists have encouraged educators to consider individual differences in preparing lessons and units. Individualized instruction provides for this situation. This instructional strategy takes many forms—packages, programmed instruction, and independent learning. Packages, whether teacher-prepared or commercial, usually contain objectives, learning activities, self-evaluations, and a final evaluation. Students obtain packets from teachers and in most cases work on their own in the classroom, learning resource center, and library.[21] Teachers are available for consultation, small group work, and correction of papers. Some variations exist, such as, computer terminals. Likewise, programmed instruction takes many forms. Generally the following characteristics are common, and material is presented in sequential, small steps, with self-pacing and immediate feedback of results on the questions spaced throughout the materials. Machines have frequently been used in programmed instruction. Often, however, it is teacher-made materials and commercially purchased textbooks that provide learning experiences. Nearly all educators have incorporated into their lessons and units provision for independent study because of its flexibility. This method permits field and library research for all students as well as excellent enrichment opportunities for the gifted learner.

As previously stated, a pre-assessment of students often reveals who has been exposed to individualized learning. In the general mode of individualized learning, independent study is best suited for minicourses. This is because of the somewhat sedentary noninteractive nature of the others (e.g., packages, programmed instruction) that runs counter to the concept of the minicourse program. Students or groups of students in consort with teachers can design lively independent studies which can often be presented to the class. However, in some cases programmed instructional materials may be useful where a mini cannot be offered because too few students wish to enroll. These students can use programmed instruction under the part-time guidance of a teacher.

e) Field Based

One of the characteristics of the minicourse movement, field based learnings, can have a very positive effect upon students, teacher, schools, and the community. Ross Engel and David Weller of Iowa State University have argued field based learnings are one of the prime justifications for mini's: "The mini-course concept provides the opportunity for improving school-community communication and, consequently, offers a fine medium for public relations."[22] Allan Glatthorn analyzes the situation:

> For decades past, the school and community have existed in an uneasy and unhealthy relationship. They were seen as two separate worlds, with the wall between them breached only periodically by sporadic attempts at "community involvement." Consequently, they often perceived each other as adversaries competing for dollars, space and children's loyalties.[23]

Instructors can integrate community experiences and teach field-based courses. These types of learnings appear relevant to students as they provide real world experiences. Travel, career education work, volunteer service, and community study exist as just some of the possibilities available. Well-organized goal oriented field trips of varying lengths offer an excellent opportunity for the instructor to integrate visits into their courses. Social studies classes can visit historical sites; science groups might examine local ecology; and art students can sketch local architecture. Schools may wish to arrange career education opportunities, placing students in positions to expand their awareness of future jobs and even gain job experience. Suburban, middle class schools can provide positions in blue collar and unskilled positions that will help make their students aware of and appreciate persons and occupations unfamiliar to them.

If there exists difficulty in placement, volunteer service offers an alternative which can encourage a selfless regard for others needed in today's society. Libraries, schools (tutoring), local government offices, senior citizens institutions, and hospitals (health clinics) constitute just a sample of the possibilities. Students could receive minicourse credit for planned volunteer service, and teachers to maximize learning need to provide a follow-up to permit students to reflect upon their experiences.

The community exists as a rich laboratory frequently ignored and overlooked for its informal learning potential. The following community experiences can be integrated into minicourses:

- Interview senior citizens who can describe town life when they were in school (oral history)

- Study of the future growth of the community including population shifts, zoning, and building plans

- Examine prices between stores on the same items (comparative pricing)

- Photograph the oldest buildings in town

- Visit a nearby cemetery and study life expectancies over time by analyzing grave stones

- Observe street names and hypothesize the reason for the name and research the reason

- Graph the crime rate over time; make some predictions for the future; make suggestions to curtail crime.

Teachers should not forget that the community can come to the school in the form of minicourse instructors and guest lecturers with special knowledge and skills. The success of all these programs requires very careful planning to provide assurance for students; to avoid problems that will reflect badly upon the school, the teacher, and the students; and to construct a learning experience that will aid students to achieve the objectives mutually planned by them and the teacher. The use of the community as an instructional strategy deserves the careful consideration of all of those connected with a minicourse program.

29

f) Demonstration

The demonstration, usually thought of more as a method than a strategy, has particular significance for minicourses, specifically the shorter ones. Examination of present offerings shows many that concentrate upon the instructor demonstrating a skill and then students practicing it. Courses of this genre carry titles such as, "How to Refinish Wood Furniture," "Meditation and Relaxation," "Candle Making," "Modeling," "Trampoline for Fun," "Basic Auto Mechanics for Women," "Clock Repairs," "Vegetable Planting," and "First Aid." Instructors should be well organized and provide handouts of terminology and of the step-by-step process involved in the craft or skill—accompanying drawings would be valuable. The practicing of the demonstration before a group of volunteers can serve to approximate the time involved in the presentation. Frequently, the person with a special skill will proceed too quickly in explaining the how-to techniques to others, assuming that the learner knows more than is the actual case. A dry-run can help to prevent some or all of this as can videotaping, filming, or slide-audio taping of the presentation in the library or learning resource center. Once students begin to practice their skills, the instructor might wish to work with small groups on a rotating basis so as to monitor progress and make necessary suggestions. Clearly, people seem to enjoy demonstrations and profit from them, and courses of this nature should continue as part of minicourse programs. Teachers may wish to solicit free materials for student use from businesses; some schools will not be able to purchase supplies, forcing students to provide their own. Most are willing to do this as they will retain the products of their labors.

g) Basic Skills

The widespread cry by the public and politicians for accountability and the dismal academic performance of some high school graduates has stirred growing interest in the basic skills.[24] To reading, writing, and arithmetic, educators generally add other basic subjects, such as, viewing, human relations, critical thinking, map reading, graph interpretation, problem solving, and speaking. While many instructors will attempt to integrate these skills into their minicourses, needs analysis (input) will undoubtedly reveal requests for courses in the basic skills. Minicourses have permitted the college bound student, traditionally following a rigid program, to take nonacademic courses. Now these students can obtain skills in areas such as the following: income tax reporting, installment buying, job acquisition (and interviewing), and typing. Generally, these had been the preserve of the business and general student. Minicourses in these and other areas should find an audience among college preparatory program students. All students can profit from "Reading Improvement," "Building Writing Skills," "Logical Thinking" and similar courses; their specific design would involve skill practice. One of the criticisms of alternative and innovative programs like minicourses often focuses on their overreaction to "relevancy" and the superficial nature of these courses. The integration of basic skills objectives into mini's and the offerings of courses specifically to build and practice a skill quickly silences this criticism—which many times is justified. Skills-development instruction constitutes one of the most difficult forms of teaching, which partially accounts for its absence in many schools. Surveys of English classes have shown that only about 15 percent of course time has been devoted to writing composition. It is also difficult for the student who may have a mental block and needs the challenge of high interest motivation methods. Self-actualization in an urban industrial society requires schools to furnish basic skills: speaking skills to the union vice-president, writing skills for consumers desiring to compose complaint letters, and interpersonal skills to help everyone work amiably with fellow employees. The obligation of educators to incorporate skills-development strategies into their courses is quite clear.

Although not thought of in these terms, psychomotor skills justifiably can be classified as basic skills—particularly in view of the increased leisure time available to Americans. Health statistics remind us that we need more exercise and greater opportunities to reduce stress. Most students have opportunities for exposure to lifetime sports programs; however, few have the time for in-depth practice and instruction. Minicourses in the lifetime sports skills area serve to expose students to these sports and provide time to initiate their development. Such a program might offer the following, among others: "Introduction to Badminton," "Advanced Tennis Skills," "Intermediate Back Backing." Likewise, other activity oriented offerings may carry the following titles, among numerous possibilities: "Water Painting: Introductory Level," "Antiquing Furniture," "Model Shipbuilding."

Educators have quickly found that basic skills strategies offer something of value to everyone regardless of ability, grade level, and interest. These skills provide prerequisite knowledge and abilities important to self-fulfillment in today's society as well as promoting confidence in the schools by the community as well as the graduates.

Organization of Groups

While there is no clear standard for group size, the level and category of objectives provide some guidelines. If the category falls into the affective domain, then group size will be smaller than is conventionally used. Research on classroom groups has consistently found "that a positive social climate . . . enhances students' self-esteem and their academic performances." With minicourse programs that traditionally emphasize affective learnings, class sizes should be kept at a minimum. The following questions can serve as aids:

1. Which objectives can be reached by the learner on her or his own?
2. Which objectives can be achieved through interaction among the learners themselves?
3. Which objectives can be achieved through formal presentation by the teacher and through interaction between the learner and the teacher?[25]

The answers to the above will not only provide clues to strategies but also to space, time, resources, and group size. For example, a prominant college professor, local personality, or author might offer a three-day mini where the objectives are largely cognitive. The course may take the lecture-discussion format and group size may reach over a hundred. A local TV newscaster may attract many to such a course. However, because of the action orientation, demonstrations, and the close personal contact between teacher and students, class sizes should fall around fifteen. Social psychologists tell teachers that group processes have an important effect on the learning process. According to Richard and Patricia Schmuck:

> There are several reasons why group processes in the classroom have become a primary concern of most educators. The increasing complexity of social conditions and large concentrations of people have brought to the forefront the need for and importance of learning to work effectively in groups. . . . The classroom is not a depersonalized setting; it abounds with emotion between teachers and students and between students and their peers. . . . In some classrooms, the learning process is enhanced by peer relations that actively support a productive learning atmosphere; in others, it is inhibited by peer relations.[26]

Schmuck and Schmuck further report:

> *The data on size give clear evidence that the necessary ingredients for learning—involvement and participation—are not encouraged by large and impersonal schools.*[27]

The minicourse approach can offset the impersonal negative environment found in some schools or reinforce the positive climates of others. Minicourse designers and instructors, in light of the importance of group size and the importance it has to personal growth and development, should devote considerable time to holding classes to a reasonable size—particularly in courses which emphasize affective objectives. The minicourse program in many schools exists as a reaction to the lack of concern in schools for values, attitudes, and emotions. Teachers must not overlook the relationship of group size to the continued success of this curricular offering. Charles Wiese in "Mini-courses: New Spark for Student Enrichment" suggests that "Mini-courses can bring students and faculty closer together by providing an informal setting where they can learn to know each other."[28]

Allocation of Time

The determination for time utilization will closely follow the approach of the school. Generally, two forms exist: (1.) Normal time periods used with nine- or ten-week courses (at the intermediate and secondary level these will fall between 40 and 50 minutes, and modifications because of field trips, community activities, and similar events will vary this standard time format on occasion). (2.) Shorter time periods of one-day to one-week arrangements (times will vary with the teachers' answers to the three questions in the preceding section and as school scheduling permits). For example, Stevenson High School in Prairie View, Illinois, used a "minimum" of two hours daily in a one-week program. New Trier East High School used a "maximum" of three hours daily in a three-day program.[29] At both schools, students could stay longer if they wanted to attend open sessions—activities like theater workshops, films, speakers, and panels that ran throughout the day. Of course, the scheduling of some mini's determines the time periods, but those scheduled during lunch periods, study halls, and the final period of the day are set to fit the pre-established time allocation. Most teachers of courses realize that in some cases (regardless of the conclusions reached by them after examining objectives, content, and strategies) administrative philosophy and practical constraints will not permit flexibility of time schedules. These cases require very precise planning for achievement of objectives and positive student response. Frequently, teachers will respond to such challenges by working with colleagues and students to permit lengthier time sequences for particular lessons as required by guest presentations, field trips, simulations, or demonstrations.

Allocation of Space

Much the same as with time, the allocation of learning space varies with objectives, content, teaching strategies, and administrative scheduling patterns. In terms of minicourses, consideration must be given toward providing space or making arrangements for independent study, demonstrations, small group activities, and simulations. Large group areas for guest presentations exist in most schools and can be easily arranged; however, small group spaces and demonstration may prove difficult. Prudence suggests early reservation of any wanted space as similar demands for certain areas will be common during the minicourse program period. During the meeting with the librarian for the discussion of resources and instructional materials, arrangements should be made for independent and group study projects. Many libraries presently provide study carrels and small group rooms for semi-isolation and privacy. For the student preparing a written or oral presentation, these rooms can be very helpful. Because of the various strategies employed in teaching today, instructors will need to employ the concurrent appropriate learning spaces. Again, teachers must work together with students in locating and preparing for maximum efficiency of available space. No one should be shocked or surprised to find "Small Farm Planning" scheduled in the women's gym or "Vegetarianism" in the left front section of the auditorium, or even "Slide Rule Use" in the office of the mathematics department chairperson. Space utilization and efficiency of instruction are intimately tied, and teachers must devote the requisite time necessary for the planning in this category.

Selection of Resources

Introduction

Beginning during the mid 1960's and continuing almost untrammeled to the present has been the tremendous growth of instructional resources. The situation for educators has changed from "I hope I can find something on First American Indians" to "Which booklets, films, sound filmstrips, handouts, etc., should I use with my advanced six graders?" However, teachers of minicourses will need to do some searching to locate appropriate resources, because of the generally nontraditional nature of minicourses. Some difficulty may occur initially because of the unfamiliarity of the instructor with materials in the specific minicourse area; however, this should not prove much of a problem because of the abundance (frequent overabundance) of resources available for each general subject area.

Teaching techniques, as suggested earlier, closely follow the action theme associated with the movement. Michael Steirer, Assistant Principal of Elyria High School in Ohio, summarizes the situation: "We do not emphasize textbook instruction; the students concentrate on learning from first-hand experience.[30] Robert Hayward echoes this: "Their requests for topics emphasized 'doing' subjects such as poetry, writing, film making, scuba diving and dramatics, but a surprising number of students indicated an interest in religion, philosophy, and contemporary problems."[31] Consequently, teachers need to be flexible to meet the great variety of student interests. The following research findings by Daniel S. Parkinson show this:

> Methods used in minicourses are characterized by extensive variety. Over 80% of the schools reported the use of discussion, independent study, lecture, recitation, and small-group work. Over 70% reported use of oral reports, resource speakers and audiovisual aids. Over half of the schools reported use of field trips, library or media center work, cooperative planning between teacher and student, and term papers.[32]

The eclectic approach continues to find more adherents in the teaching profession because of two reasons. Different instructional objectives require different approaches, and varying classroom learning experiences adds diversity and variety to the course and maintains student interest. Clearly this format should form the instructional basis of every minicourse.

Choosing Instructional Materials

The following hierarchy can prove a useful tool and reference as teachers examine their own objectives and plan the students' learning experiences.

CONCRETE EXPERIENCES

1. *Real Life Experiences.* Interviewing an eye witness, handling artifacts, performing an experiment, a trip to a French restaurant, talking with an elected public servant.
2. *Physical Involvement with Artificial or Simulated Experience.* Learning games or simulations, role playing and re-enacting events, models of the real thing.
3. *Direct Perception of Experiences (Actual Observation).* Touring an exhibit, watching a jury trial or legislature, field trip to observe play, observing demonstrations and viewing finished products.
4. *Indirect Perception of Experience (Audio/Visual Representation).* Television, sound films, filmstrips and slide presentations, video tape.
5. *Visual Representation of Experiences.* Silent films (usually 8mm), slides, filmstrips, photographs, bulletin board charts and pictures, transparencies.
6. *Audio Representation of Experiences.* Audio tapes and records of events, speeches, radio.
7. *Reading Verbal Description of Experience.* Textbooks, handouts, paperback book accounts, notes on overhead projector and chalkboard.
8. *Hearing Verbal Description of Experience.* In-person lecture description or on record or tape.[33]

ABSTRACT EXPERIENCES

The above activities, referred to as "Dale's Cone of Experience," arranged in a hierarchial format, suggests that teachers should aim for high level activities. While this seems commendable, it may not always be feasible or educationally sound. In terms of the earlier suggestions, teachers will wish to vary learning experiences because of a desire to add variety to the classroom and because different objectives will require different student responses to achieve them. The author strongly suggests that where possible, teachers use more than one experience in instruction. For example, in the early sessions of a course entitled "Silk Screening" not only should students watch demonstrations, but they should also receive handouts (dittoed sheets) explaining the process in a step-by-step fashion. Perhaps they should have the opportunity to view a sound filmstrip presentation in the library during free time. In terms of Dale's paradigm, minicourses generally operate at the higher levels (frequently level one), which may partially explain their success.

Appropriateness, cost, and quality exist as important factors in choosing instructional material; however, sometimes they cannot be considered unless availability is met.

Sources of Instructional Materials

For some years in teaching, availability of teaching materials determined the method the instructor would use. Recently, as the profession moves toward a more systematic and efficient approach toward learning, objectives have generally determined student learning activities. Availability of materials and the willingness of teachers to produce their own classroom items have considerably contributed to this trend.

The following general guides are offered as suggestions to locate media and materials:

Guides to Newer Educational Media: Films, Filmstrips, Kinescopes, Phonodiscs, Programmed Instructional Materials, Slides, Transparencies and Videotapes. American Library Association, 50 East Huron Street, Chicago, Illinois 60611.

Educators' Guide to Free Films, Educators' Guide to Free Filmstrips, Educators' Guide to Free and Inexpensive Teaching Materials. Educators' Progress Service, Randolph, Wisconsin.

NICEM Indexes: *Index to 16mm Educational Films, Index to 8mm Motion Cartridges, Index to 35mm Filmstrips, Index to Educational Records, Index to Audiotapes, Index to Video Tapes, Index to Educational Overhead Transparencies.* R.R. Bowker, 1180 Avenue of the Americas, New York, N.Y.

Sources of Free and Inexpensive Pictures for the Classroom, Sources of Free Travel Posters, So You Want to Start A Picture File. The Bruce Miller Publications, Riverside, California.

Sources of Free and Inexpensive Pictures for the Classroom. Educators' Progress Service, Randolph, Wisconsin.

Selected Free Materials for Classroom Teachers. Fearon Publishers, 2165 Park Boulevard, Palo Alto, California.

Textbooks in Print. R. R. Bowker Company, New York.

Guide to Simulation Games for Education and Training. Information Resources, Lexington, Massachusetts.

Programmed Learning: A Bibliography of Programs and Presentation Devices. Carl Hendershot, 4114 Ridgewood Drive, Bay City, Michigan.

Educational Television Motion Pictures. (catalog) Net Film Service, Audio-Visual Center, Indiana University, Bloomington, Indiana 47401.

Additional suggestions appear elsewhere in this book; also, general ideas can be obtained from the sample minicourses bibliography.[34] Librarians, audio-visual directors, and curriculum coordinators must act as resource locators for teachers. William Swenson suggests the following procedures:

> The department chairman or supervisor should now actively coordinate and support their efforts by providing catalogs, information

and specific suggestions for literary materials, possible audio-visual supportive materials, articles in literary journals that pertain to specific course areas, while keeping each person aware of the department goals and objectives of the entire mini-course/electives program.[35]

While Swenson's ideas are somewhat passé on what constitutes teaching materials, his point on their acquisition is well made.

No single teaching material holds magical powers in terms of student learning; happily, the minicourse program contains built-in designs which tap those objectives, strategies, and techniques that students seem to love.

Evaluation of Performance

With a systematic approach to teaching minicourses, two types of evaluations take place—course evaluation and student evaluation. Answers to the first provide areas for course modification, which in some cases can take place immediately if the mini is offered several times a year.

The instructor must perform an evaluation, even if grades are not to be given as in cases of the shorter mini's, to obtain data for revision and refinement and to determine if the course meets the original goals that were established. Of course, often a school-wide survey soliciting input for total program modification will be conducted.

Some teachers will find this evaluation task to be somewhat difficult because of the number of affective objectives, high level cognitive objectives, and psychomotor objectives not normally part of their experience.

Criterion Referenced Tests

Recently, teachers have shown considerable interest in measuring student performance against the instructional objectives, i.e., Did the learner master the objective? Traditionally, educators have used norm referenced measures—evaluating one learner in relation to another. In terms of the approach of this book, the use of criterion referenced measures is strongy encouraged. Well-constructed objectives will facilitate the construction of this form of test item because of the close relationship between them. This type item is also suggested for the pre-assessment of students. In terms of the minicourse, this approach has several advantages:

1. Assessment of the learner's attainment of the objectives provides data to the teacher. Analysis of this information provides clues to areas that need improvement. Many times, these can be quickly

implemented, particularly if the course is offered several times a year.

2. Student grades (where given) are a function of the student's individual performance and not of the class as a whole. Learners' grades will be a result of their mastery of the objectives and not of how well they form relative to the rest of the class. Unfortunately, sometimes in the past, if a student took a course with a "smart" group, he/she may obtain a "B" (or the reverse: a student taking a course with a "slow" group may obtain an "A"). Consequently, his/her grade was a function of the semester they took the course. This can be a serious problem because of the number of times some mini's are offered and the number of sections in which it is offered. Surely, teachers will want to avoid this.

3. Because many minicourses are skill related and "doing" experiences, evaluation of the mastery of the instructional objective seems a natural procedure. For example, in a mini such as "Karate" ("the students will learn the basics of self-defense techniques") or "Office Experience" (". . . will gain good experience in routine, equipment and procedures"), teachers (as well as those who originally suggested the course, the input group) will want to know if, in fact, what was supposed to take place actually took place.

Criterion referenced measurement holds many promises for the improvement of teaching through a systematic approach.[36]

Constructing Evaluative Measures

The following section is not meant to provide the basic foundation of an educator's knowledge but rather to offer some suggestions for constructing useful test items for minicourses.

Measurement in the affective domain often seems to teachers a difficult if not impossible task. Fortunately, there exist some procedures helpful to teachers:

1. Observation, direct and indirect. Simply just watching students reactions and behaviors and unobstrusively checking to see if changes or interests have taken place.
   Example. After concluding a minicourse, observe the reaction to the following question: "If anyone wishes to help me teach and plan this course the next time it is offered, please see me after class." Or following a course on First American "Indians," count how many students checked out books on the topic.

2. Likert Scale. Most persons are familiar with this simple but useful tool.
   Example. The field trip to the First American reservation was a valuable experience (circle one): strongly agree   agree   neutral   disagree   strongly disagree.

Several of this kind of question can easily be constructed, administered and scored.

3. Semantic differential. Again, this is an easy to use tool familiar to most people, but until recently, rarely used in the classroom.[37]

   Example. Please indicate your reaction to the concept by placing an X on the appropriate space:

First Americans

Smart	————	————	————	————	————	Dull
Slow	————	————	————	————	————	Fast

The Likert scale and the semantic differential can be given prior to the course to obtain pre-test and post-test measures of attitudinal change. Additional information on these techniques exist in most recent books on teaching methods and evaluation. The reader may wish also to consult David Krathwohl's *Taxonomy of Educational Objectives—Handbook II: The Affective Domain*,[38] which provides not only a scheme for writing objectives but also an explanation of the levels of attitudinal internalization that are helpful in assessing affective behavior.

Until recently, schools have largely concerned themselves with cognitive growth. Tests have reflected this emphasis, and educators' experience and skills in this area are quite extensive and good. Two suggestions for minicourse instructors are to use (1.) essay questions and (2.) higher level test items. The encouragement of creative thinking on examinations can be made easier by the above suggestions. Benjamin Bloom's *Taxonomy of Educational Objectives—Handbook I: The Cognitive Domain*[39] offers excellent advice for teachers wishing to do this:

High Level

6. *Evaluation*. Questions at this level require making a judgment based upon a standard or criteria determined by the learner. The answer must be documented and justified.

   Example: Which of the following two men is the better author: Edgar Allen Poe or Ambrose Bierce?

5. *Synthesis*. Requires putting together an excellent communication oral or written to form a new pattern of communication.

   Example: Prepare a speech predicting the future of arts and crafts in America.

4. *Analysis*. Requires the breaking down of the communication into its parts. The student might identify the constituent elements in an advertisement.

   Example: Analyze this politician's speech to see which electoral groups (pressure groups) he/she is appealing to for votes.

3. *Application.* Requires the use of abstractions in particular and concrete situations.
   Example: Predict the probable effect of introducing a change into a biological situation that previously was at equilibrium, e.g., a fish tank.

2. *Comprehension.* Requires the understanding of a communication.
   Example: Examine this political cartoon and explain its meaning.

1. *Knowledge.* Requires the production from memory of theories, principles, generalizations, and facts.
   Example: List the safety procedures for the changing of a tire on an automobile.

In using the above model, teachers must remember the importance of preconditions. For example, if on Tuesday, an instructor stated, "The most important, interesting, and significant aspect of what we'll see on our field trip is . . .", then asks the following test question a week later—"What do you think was the most important, interesting and significant aspect of last week's field trip," this would require simple recall, not an evaluative decision.

The in-depth concentrated nature of the mini provides the foundation to permit students to operate at higher levels of thinking. This opportunity should be encouraged by challenging, demanding questions. All learners have the ability to operate at the creative level and must be permitted to do so.

Psychomotor behavior clearly exists more in minicourse programs than in traditional offerings. Unfortunately, this domain has not experienced the development and refinement of the others. However, some guidelines for teachers do exist, and these can be helpful to those faculty members who normally do not work in the motor skill area. Vocational-technical teachers, physical education specialists, and others have experience in this area and can serve as resource people.

Robert Kibler, Larry Barker, and David Miles, authors of *Behavioral Objectives and Instruction*,[40] offer this classification:

4.00 *Speech Behaviors.* Behaviors in this category exist in public speaking, communication arts, and speech correction.
   Example: Give a three-minute lecture using coordinated gestures and body movements.

3.00 *Non-Verbal Communication Behaviors.* Behaviors in this category convey a message without the use of words—facial expressions, gestures, and bodily movements.
   Example: Show how to press a weight of 100 pounds without using the weight itself, using facial and body movements.

    2.00   *Finely Coordinated Movements.* These behaviors occur in the industrial arts, fine arts, handicrafts, and similar areas which are frequently the basis for minicourses.
Example: (a) Show an example of jewelry that you have—copper enameled by hand; (b) Demonstrate how to hitch a recreation vehicle or boat trailer to an automobile.

    1.00   *Gross Body Movements.* Movements of entire limbs alone or in connection with other parts of the body characterizes this category.
Example: Throw a softball over the plate once in three chances from the pitcher's mound.

Teachers will find it helpful to use checksheets of their objectives when they are observing psychomotor skills or examining objectives of art produced by the learner.

Evaluation constitutes a very important part of any instructional system. Learners many times judge the course and the instructor by the evaluation procedures used. Consequently, if faculty members want to maintain the positive attitude researchers tell us that students have toward teachers and toward the course, then evaluation deserves time and thought. In fact, the success of the entire minicourse system presented in this book depends upon proper evaluation.

Analysis of Feedback

Successful teachers have long used both formal and informal procedures to improve their teaching. A teacher may re-explain a difficult procedure as a result of the frowns on students' faces, or a teacher may review the content or a given skill area as a result of the answers to a test question.

Feedback should be collected to evaluate a course, and should be examined especially by those who suggested, designed, and taught the course. Chart 1 in this chapter details this important analysis of feedback. It is possible that the feedback data will suggest course elimination, re-emphasis, or a more advanced treatment. In most cases, however, simple modification will be the only adjustment necessary.

In this era of accountability and budget-consciousness, there are many attempts to make learning more efficient and teaching more humanistic. Teachers should use many systematic procedures and practical ideas in achieving success in today's classroom. Minicourses seem to contain an innate mechanism for success; proper planning almost guarantees it.

4.   Studying Others' Minicourses

The majority of minicourses developed and offered to date have been in the humanities—particularly history, the social sciences, English, and literature. Many schools permit minicourses only in the social studies and English (communication arts). It is difficult to know the exact reason for this restriction, although these disciplines more easily lend themselves to minicourse organization; whereas, other disciplines may follow a sequence of increasing difficulty and require more basic foundation prerequisites for the study of special areas. It should be mentioned, however, that several schools do offer mini's in all or almost all subject areas.

Frequently, these courses in English and the social studies are characterized by the interdisciplinary approach (e.g., "Sports Literature," "Cultural Anthropology,") and the exotic (e.g., "History of Witchcraft," "Writing Science Fiction"), which can partially account for their appearance and success. Their unusualness does not mean these courses are inherently frillish or intellectual mavericks since they are legitimate subdivisions of the main discipline or intersections of two or more bodies of knowledge. That history and English rank lowest in student interest has been a contributing factor to the direction minicourses have taken. A Louis Harris poll[1] on schools in 1969 found these two subjects as the most boring to students, and 1969 can generally be regarded as the initial year of the minicourse movement. The call for motivating courses must not only be answered by what interests the student but also by solidly academic courses that contribute to knowledge as well as skills.

The two minicourses that follow in the next chapters have been chosen as models because they are within the humanities and are typical of minicourses that have been and will be offered. Additionally, they are flexible enough to have their length varied and diverse enough to permit content emphasis as the local situation requires. In this way, they achieve their specific instructional objectives. Even though minicourses are sufficiently novel in terms of the traditional offerings in school, there is an availability of instructional materials for these courses that helps to illustrate what the classroom teacher must do to prepare a successful minicourse.

The two model minicourses (or variations of them) hopefully may be adopted by teachers. The outlines, materials, ideas, and annotated bibliographies that follow should offer enough suggestions and information to provide a significant basis from which the course can be built without too much additional research and course development. These two mini's have another particularly important asset—easy modification to grade level. With certain obvious, but not too numerous, variations, these courses can serve the primary, middle school, junior high, senior high, and, even, college student.

In analyzing these courses, arguments in their favor become obvious; and, hopefully, the reader will become convinced of their value, their content, and their assortment of methodological approaches and instructional approaches. Perhaps these suggestions will eventually serve as ammunition in convincing curriculum committees and students. Another value of these model minicourses, and one that has characterized the movement, is the possible latitude of who may teach. "Sports Literature," for example, may be taught by an English teacher or physical educator but might likewise be taught by a physics teacher who is a former track star or a superintendent who is an avid baseball fan. Consider also the possibility for guest presentations—coaches, players, local sports writers. "America's Maritime Heritage," exemplifys this flexibility quite well—even the school maintenance person might have World War II naval experiences to share.

The examples that follow represent two ways of examining and organizing a body of knowledge so that it can be most easily imparted to and best retained by the learner. Studying minicourses other than these would also be helpful.

5.   Minicourse 1: "America's Maritime Heritage"

Introduction

The importance and influence of the sea has frequently been forgotten, not only by the layperson but by historians, social scientists, and educators.

A moment's reflection should remind teacher and student of the role the seas and inland waters have played and continue to play in the lives of peoples and destinies of nations. In a world in which water covers nearly three fourths of the earth's surface, water has naturally contributed to the development of humankind in many ways. Life began in the sea; it has served as the cradle for the early civilizations, and has existed as a food source as well as a highway for travel, trade, and cultural interchange. Historically the sea has been closely involved with the rise and fall of societies, cultures, and nations. The Biblical story of Moses and his crossing of the Red Sea forms an important part of Judaic-Christian tradition. Important naval battles (e.g., the defeat of the Spanish Armada by England) have changed the course of history. Nations have taken dangerous risks in pursuing foreign policies to obtain more favorable strategic holdings (e.g., Russia's "Windows to the West"). Other societies have placed themselves on the pages of history because of their conquest of the sea (e.g., Phoenicians, Vikings). The survival of the island nations and those countries bordering the sea has been related to how well they have used the water which entirely or partially surrounds them. Japan, prior to embarking on an aggressive foreign policy, strengthened its navy considerably. Today, the Soviet Union spends considerable sums of money expanding its commercial fishing industry and merchant shipping as well as its huge navy, and these policies have one purpose—to contribute to strengthening the country as a superpower. Recent conferences dealing with the future of the oceans and the law of the sea demonstrate the importance water will play as nations in the future vie for the riches of the oceans.

Considering the importance of the sea, it is unfortunate that America's maritime heritage has been seriously slighted. In fact, examination of textbooks, course outlines, and curriculum guides makes it painfully obvious that this topic receives little, if any, attention. In fact, if one were to examine certain periods of American history by using present curriculum materials, it would be easy to arrive at the conclusion that the United States is a landlocked nation.[1] This is quite ironic as it was the sea that enabled the discovery, colonization, and development of our nation as we know it today. The level of our standard of living, our position as a world power, and much of our cultural heritage are closely linked to the sea. The existence of the present situation is somewhat difficult to understand considering the romantic and colorful nature of the maritime tradition. This heritage encompasses such areas as art (seascapes), crafts (figure carving, scrimshaw, model shipbuilding), architecture (ships, lighthouses), music (sea chanteys), undersea treasure hunting (sunken ships of the Spanish main), sea monsters (sharks and other fish), sea legends and tales (mermaids, Bermuda Triangle), and literature and films (*Moby Dick, Jaws*).

Because the maritime enterprise has shaped much of our culture, let us consider language as an example of its impact upon American society. Proponents of Frederick Jackson Turner's frontier thesis have pointed to Americanisms such as "shooting from the hip" and being "trigger happy" as partial documentation for their position that the landed frontier experience shaped America and its institutions. If the long-expected visitor from Mars should arrive in the United States and perform an analysis of the language, the visitor would conclude, however, that the country's inhabitants were essentially a seafaring people. As language is a mirror of a country's history and habits, our maritime experience has left an imprint upon the nation. In fact, sea talk has become so assimilated and ingrained into the language that its origin is often overlooked and rarely reflected upon. Consider the following examples: "first rate," "batten down the hatches," "castaway," "a fish story," "to give a wide berth," "to take the wind out of his sails," "to run a taut ship," "blubber," "to carry on," "ironclad," "full speed ahead," "on deck," "to give a clean bill of health," "to make headway," "bunk," and "loose ends."[2] These constitute but a small sample of the maritime terms in our daily usage.

Recent activities may help to focus attention on this area: "Operation Sail" which culminated in New York City on July 4, 1976; the Panama Canal controversy, the "200-mile limit" question, water shortage and pollution, and the issue of naval superiority.

Content

Once the decision has been made through a needs analysis or by convincing the curriculum committee that a course in this area would be both educational and valuable, there exists a wealth of content for the teacher wishing to discuss the contribution of the maritime enterprise to the development of America. Units or short minicourses could develop around the following themes:

1. The shipbuilding industry (active in the country for over 300 years) could be studied, possibly highlighting certain periods and types of ships, e.g., the square riggers of New England, the monitors of Civil War fame, the romantic clipper ships, the Liberty ships of World War II, and the nuclear submarines or pleasure boats of today. Such an investigation might also examine the effects of the Industrial Revolution upon ship-building towns and their workers.

2. The literature of the sea provides a diverse and highly interesting topic that may take many directions. In poetry: Philip Freneau's "The British Prison-Ship," Oliver W. Holmes's "Old Ironsides," Henry Wadsworth Longfellow's "The Building of the Ship," Walt Whitman's "Song for All Seas, All Ships," and "O Captain, My Captain!" In drama: Eugene O'Neill's "Thirst" and "Anna Christie." In fiction: Robert Louis Stevenson's *Treasure Island*, Jack London's *The Sea Wolf*, C. S. Forester's *The Captain from Connecticut*, Herman Wouk's *The Caine Mutiny*. In nonfiction: Richard H. Dana's *Two Years Before the Mast*, Owen Chase's *Shipwreck of the Whaleship Essex*, and Charles Wilkes's *Narrative of the Exploring Expedition*. These readings can cover every interest and teaching objective. A course could even be initiated by Peter Benchley's film *Jaws*.

3. A historical and contemporary case study could be made of a major or minor port analyzing its growth and the development of the trade specialties peculiar to that port. For example: New Orleans, Chicago, San Francisco, Hoboken, N.J., Chester, Pa., and Port Arthur, Tex. In addition to examining the commercial aspects of port life, teachers and students could consider the geographic and economic requisites for the establishment of a port—using a multidisciplinary approach.

4. The fishing industry would make an interesting study and could be examined in terms of the inland waters as well as the coasts and oceans. Other approaches could include the contemporary international problems regarding fishing rights and the effects of off-shore drilling and nuclear power plants upon the catch of fish.

5. The development of naval technology might prove a valuable and interesting topic by concentrating on a particular era. For

example, the Civil War was a period of rapid technological change; the development of the monitors by the Union and the development of the submarines and mines by the Confederacy could provide a provocative content.

6. An investigation could be conducted of the nation's maritime trading industry. This could focus on its development to its present state, examining the domestic trade of the inland waters and canals as well as their foreign trade. It may be most useful in this regard to focus upon a few particular trade items of general interest (such as, petroleum, heavy machinery, or agriculture) or on an item of local significance.

7. Frequently local and state history can provide content for a unit on maritime studies. Obviously some states and localities bordering on bodies of water are rich in maritime history, while others away from water would have less of a heritage. However, a little digging may discover a ship named after the state or local community, or a resident who had been a famous ship captain or naval hero. (During World War II, Kansas had the highest per capita volunteer rate for the Navy.)

8. The life of people serving in the Coast Guard is frequently recognized as one of the interesting maritime occupations. A study of the Coast Guard's activities would prove both enjoyable and enlightening.

9. An anthropology-oriented unit might study the movement of peoples to the New World, contrasting the different theories on the origin of the first Americans. It might also analyze the Alaskan land bridge, the possible existence of the "lost continent" of Atlantis, and the theories of Thor Heyerdahl (See his book *The Ra Expeditions*).

10. A short unit on pirates can prove to be not only of great interest to students but it can serve as a springboard to other related topics. For example, there are contemporary pirates in the drug trade, and there are the historical pirates of the Caribbean.

Additional miniunits could be built around some of the more exotic topics related to oceanic education, such as, ferry boats, whaling, smuggling, lighthouses, sea monsters, treasure hunting, arts and crafts, seafood, and underwater tunnels. The subject matter is adaptable to many disciplines and subject area specialties.

Methodology

American maritime heritage offers opportunities for all teachers regardless of which instructional strategy they might prefer. For teachers interested in using inquiry or discovery strategies, maritime studies offer unlimited opportunities. The conflicting analysis of the reasons accounting for the Pearl Harbor incident should stimulate students to critical-thinking discussions that require evaluative judgments. The readings, excerpts from Rear Admiral Robert A. Theobald's *USN, The Final Secret of Pearl Harbor* and selected passages from Samuel Eliot Morison's *The Two-Ocean War,* provide contrasting explanations for the event. Theobald in support of Admiral Kimmel builds the case that President Roosevelt encouraged the attack by Japan; Morison takes a different position regarding U.S. foreign policy.

Another example that can be used as a basis for teaching about historiography (conflicting explanations of a single event) is the recent book *Lusitania,* by Colin Simpson, which states that British Intelligence encouraged and welcomed the attack and disaster in order to bring the United States into the War against Germany. (Professor Thomas Bailey of Stanford University has a work in progress contradicting Simpson's thesis.) Similarly, Alfred Thayer Mahan's theories (*The Influence of Sea Power Upon History*) can be contrasted with the theories, philosophies, and interpretations of others (Spengler, Marx, Toynbee).

Classic maritime history primary sources, such as Richard H. Dana's *Two Years Before the Mast* and the both humorous and serious first-person account of the attack upon Pearl Harbor by Tai Sing Loo, "How Happen I Were in Pearl Harbor" (*Shipmate,* December 1972), provide valuable insights into the era in which they were written. In addition, contrasting accounts of an event serve as a focal point for an examination of the recording of history. One such example is the account of the Battle of Manila Bay. Lieutenant Carlos G. Calkins, a participant, wrote his version of the battle for the *U.S. Naval Institute Proceedings* (See annotated bibliography). Following its publication Admiral Dewey quickly responded:

> The article has appeared in publication which is understood to have the official sanction of the Department, and as it contains as facts conflicting with my official reports, I consider it necessary that the Department will request the Naval Institute to publish in its next issue my official report of the Battle of Manila Bay, which is absolutely correct in all essentials.[3]

Admiral Dewey's letter and official account of the battle appeared in the next issue of the *Proceedings* (September 1899). Surely these accounts form the basis of an interesting and useful lesson in the study of the writing of history and demonstrate the value of primary sources to the historian.

America's rich maritime heritage provides content for the teaching approach and inclination of every classroom teacher. We have already seen examples for those interested in inquiry and discovery learning. Import-export data, for example, could be used by students to develop generalizations concerning the changing trade relationships with the U.S. as well as the question of global interdependence. For the teacher, an abundance of political cartoons, pictures, and artifacts exist.

For the teacher emphasizing current affairs the recent expedition investigating the location of the *Monitor* provides interesting content. Shipyards, ports, naval installations, maritime museums (See annotated bibliography) are conveniently spaced throughout the nation providing field trip opportunities. Many of them have upgraded their facilities and displays during the recent years as part of Bicentennial programs. Thematic investigations may also be undertaken, such as, the development of the submarine from the drawing boards of Archimedes, da Vinci, the early prototypes, the U-boats, (such as the *Hunley* which was the first to sink a ship), and the sophisticated nuclear powered ships of today.

For the teacher or school emphasizing career education, it should be noted that there exist many opportunities in marine, maritime and related fields; the merchant marine industry alone employs over 60,000 persons (See *Occupational Outlook Handbook*, 1974–75). Any program of career education cannot afford to overlook this potential source of employment for students.

America's maritime heritage not only provides the appropriate content to develop important social studies process skills but it also provides content to motivate students—a concern of all teachers. Not only does the romantic lure of the sea have a natural appeal to students, but there are many incidents, events, and stories that can stimulate students toward reading, research, and study. Obvious examples are biographies—pirates, naval officers, explorers, and adventurers. However, one should not overlook the histories of successful ships, certain time periods (e.g., the canal era, Mississippi steamboats, clipper ships), local maritime interests (e.g., lighthouses, ferry boats) as well as maritime and naval disasters (e.g., *Andrea Doria*), sunken treasure ships, tug boats, commercial fishing, and recreational boating—to mention a few.

Interdisciplinary Possibilities

Maritime studies offers opportunities to combine many disciplines in the study of a particular topic.

Teachers wishing to emphasize anthropology can share with their students the accounts of the early exploring expeditions of the U.S. Navy. The first major U.S. Exploring Expedition, under Commander Charles Wilkes, USN, provides an abundance of information about life among the peoples of the South Pacific in his book *The Narrative of the U.S. Exploring Expedition.* Perry's *Narrative* provides similar information on Japan.

The vast literature of the sea is rich, taking the form of plays, poetry, biography, novels, short stories, nonfictional accounts, ballads, and songs. The art of the sea is also abundant. The skillful and creative teacher can build a multidisciplinary minicourse integrating the humanities (maritime literature, art, architecture, history, and the social sciences) with the economics of maritime trade, international and maritime law, the development of social justice in the U.S. Navy, the effect of geography upon maritime trade, the psychology of leadership aboard ship, and the political science of naval diplomacy.

Likewise, the marine physical sciences can contribute to an understanding of America's maritime heritage. One approach might investigate marine culture as related to the fishing industry, career education, water pollution, and the future of the oceans. Naturally, many students will be interested in the more exotic aspects of marine studies, such as, oceanography, surfing, ocean engineering, scuba and deep sea diving, which can be coordinated nicely with a combined unit on the physical sciences, the humanities, and the social sciences.

Summary

America has a rich, colorful, and important maritime heritage. With the celebration of the Bicentennial and the present interest in and the importance of the sea, maritime studies justifiably should occupy a place in the curriculum. The broad spectrum of maritime studies can provide curriculum for varied emphasis, whether process- or product-oriented or both.

In terms of minicourse programs, this area of study is particularly appropriate, combining three of the most important characteristics—flexibility of emphasis and approaches, high interest and motivational possibilities, and potential for interdisciplinary approaches.

Annotated Bibliography

Periodicals

American Neptune—a scholarly publication of the Salem Peabody Museum. Containing interesting articles of a research nature, this journal provides information on America's maritime history. Peabody Museum, Salem, Massachusetts 01970.

Oceans—publication of the Oceanic Society, "an educational and charitable non-profit membership organization." This journal, which treats current and historical topics related to maritime affairs in a readable, comprehensive fashion, contains excellent and beautifully done pictures, sketches and illustrations. 125 Independence Drive, Menlo Park, California 94025.

Sea Frontiers—a short, bi-monthly magazine with articles (illustrated) concerning advances, explorations and discoveries related to the marine sciences. Published by International Oceano-Graphic Foundation, 10 Rickenbacker Causeway, Virginia Key, Miami, Florida 33149. This organization also publishes *Sea Secrets*.

Sea Power—a publication of the Navy League, "an independent, non-profit, civilian education organization." Recent editions have contained articles (illustrated) on various aspects of maritime life—fishing industry, oceanography, shipbuilding. 818 18th Street, N.W., Washington D.C. 20036.

Shipmate—a publication of the U.S. Naval Academy Alumni Association which, along with articles relative to the alumni, contains general features on naval problems, naval developments and naval history. U.S. Naval Academy Alumni Association, Alumni House, Annapolis, Maryland 21402.

Steamboat Bill—a quarterly publication of the Steamship Historical Society of America. This journal contains short, interesting, well-illustrated features on topics such as ferry boats, Mississippi show boats and other non-naval steamships. 139 Kenyon Street, Hartford, Connecticut 06105.

United States Naval Institute Proceedings—publication of the U.S. Naval Institute, "a private, professional society for all who are interested in naval and maritime affairs." Past issues of this journal constitute an excellent primary source of maritime (especially naval) history as the periodical has recently celebrated its centennial anniversary. More recent issues deal with current maritime and naval problems. The Institute also publishes books related to naval and maritime affairs. *The Naval Review*, an annual (yearbook), reviews the year's developments and suggests future directions for the

Navy, Coast Guard and Marines and related maritime life (illustrated). U.S. Naval Institute, Annapolis, Maryland 21402.

United States Naval War College Review—a scholarly publication with articles relating not only to the Navy but also to America's maritime industry. Useful for a history of the Navy as well as for current thinking on naval problems—strategy, race relations, women in the Navy, etc. Limited distribution; however, available at many libraries. Published at the U.S. Naval War College, Newport, Rhode Island 02480.

Warship International—a magazine dealing with naval ships of all types from various nations and time periods. This periodical is highly illustrated with sketches, pictures, and plans of ships. Appearing quarterly, it is published by the Naval Records Club, 726 North Reynolds Road, Toledo, Ohio 43615.

Additional periodicals, while not devoted to maritime studies, frequently contain articles on the topic. Examples are: *American Heritage, National Geographic,* state historical journals (particularly those states with a maritime tradition), *Illustrated History, Smithsonian,* and similar journals.

Professional and Instructional Materials

Abbott, Sue Sweeney, *et al. Undersea Treasures.* Washington, D.C.: National Geographic Society, 1974. This recent book, containing over 300 pictures, illustrations and maps, provides the reader with an excellent narrative account of the riches to be obtained from the sea. The book is also unique in combining history and oceanography.

Albion, R. G. *Naval and Maritime History: An Annotated Bibliography.* (4th edition.) Mystic, Connecticut: The Marine Historical Association, 1972. An outstanding reference work listing books in all areas of maritime history (navies, safety at sea, original seafaring accounts, whaling, sea routes). This work, containing 5,000 entries, is a must for any library or curriculum materials center.

Albion, R. S. *Sea Diseases.* London: Bale. An interesting historical account of the causes and attempted cures of some of the most famous and prevalent sea diseases—dysentery, malaria, yellow fever, scurvy, typhus.

Alone in My Lobster Boat. Xerox Films 245 Long Hill Road, Middletown, Connecticut 06457. In this 16-minute color film a young boy is taught the responsibilities, the difficulties and the costs of being a Maine lobster fisherman, his father's profession.

Americana: Yankee Whaling. Audio Visual Center, Indiana University, Bloomington, Indiana 47401. A 27-minute black and white film that takes the viewer on a tour of one of the last remaining 19th Century whaling ships at Mystic, Connecticut. The film (1968) contains actual scenes of the harpooning of whales and the cutting and burning of blubber.

Annual Report of the Secretary of the Navy. Washington, D.C.: Government Printing Office. Published annually, beginning in 1798, the content provides the reader with a yearly status of the Navy—numbers, types of ships, as well as information on officers and personnel. This annual is a primary source on yearly developments in the Navy. Since 1948, contained in the Report of the Secretary of Defense; discontinued in 1970.

Barlow, A. M. *Ferryboat*. New York: Dramatist Play Service, 1974. This play details the chance meeting of two young people on a ferryboat. (One man, one woman, one exterior).

Bibliography on the History of Water Transportation, Washington, D.C.: Smithsonian Institute. This bibliography, although dated (June, 1965) exists as a fine compilation of books on ships, mariners, inventors, discoverers, ports and maritime lore.

Brassey's Naval Annual. A classic source of modern naval history (unpublished since 1886) containing factual data on the ships of all navies.

Bryant, Samuel W. *The Sea and the States: A Maritime History of the American People*. Gloucester, Massachusetts: Peter Smith, Publisher, Inc. 1947. The historical account of the development of the Navy and Merchant Marine in the United States.

Captain Stormalong. BFA Educational Media, 2211 Michigan Avenue, Santa Monica, California. This 13-minute color film details the adventures of one of America's favorite sea captains in the days of wood ships. The film covers Stormy's life from a cabin boy on a schooner until he becomes captain of the *Courser*, the largest of the clipper ships.

Catalog of United States Coast Guard Films (yearly). Washington, D.C.: U.S. Coast Guard. An annotated bibliography of 33 films available free from the U.S. Coast Guard.

Chapelle, H. I. *History of Sailing Ships*, New York: Norton, 1935. This work by a naval architect deals primarily with ship design. This outstanding work contains chapters on topics such as revenue cutters, sailing yachts and naval craft.

Chatterton, E. K. *Old Sea Paintings: The Story of Maritime Art as Depicted by the Great Masters*. 1928. New York: Dodd. This work contains many excellent paintings.

Church, W. C. *Life of John Ericson*, (2 volumes). New York: Holt. The biography of the famous architect and engineer best known for building the *Monitor*. A more recent biography is R. M. White's *Yankee from Sweden*, 1960. New York: Holt, Rinehart and Winston, Inc.

Clark, J. "Sun Ship Also Rises," *Philadelphia Magazine*. (Reprints available from Sun Ship Building, Chester, Pennsylvania) A well-done article on the state of U.S. shipbuilding, the U.S. merchant marine, and specifically the Sun Ship Building Company. The article summarizes the decline of the shipbuilding industry as well as the history of Sun Company.

Coast Guard History. Washington, D.C.: U.S. Coast Guard Public Information Division (CG-213). A short booklet summarizing the history of the Coast Guard from its days as the Revenue Marine and the Revenue Cutter Service to the present. The booklet contains many historic and contemporary illustrations.

Condliffe, J. B. *The Commerce of Nations*. New York: Norton, 1950. An economic survey of commerce through the ages as well as the conditions important for commercial actions.

Cutler, C. C. *Greyhounds of the Sea: The Story of the American Clipper*

Ship. New York: Putnam, 1930. Information on the ships of one of the most romantic periods of maritime history. Data on owners, speed, and construction.

Cutler, C. C. *Queens of the Western Ocean: The Story of America's Mail and Passenger Sailing Lines*. Annapolis, Maryland: U.S. Naval Institute, 1961. Information on the hundreds of ships that sailed the ocean and coastal waters.

Dana, R. H. *Two Years Before the Mast* (1840). New York: Signet Classics, 1964. One of the great classics of maritime life aboard ship. Dana interrupted his studies at Harvard to ship aboard a Boston brig to California. His commentary upon California made the book a best seller at the time of its initial publication; his commentary of life aboard ship made it a classic.

Debenham, F. *Discovery and Exploration: An Atlas History of Man's Journeys into the Unknown*. Toronto: Doubleday, 1960. A useful geographical reference containing many illustrations, maps, chronological tables. This book suitable for library purchase. Covers discovery and exploration on six continents.

Dodge, S. *The American Neptune*. Cambridge: Harvard University Press, 1972. A collection of scholarly, interesting and authoritative articles taken from the *American Neptune*. These well-selected articles represent a cross-section of American Maritime and Naval History.

Erie Canal. BFA Educational Media. The history of the canal is traced through the use of old photographs and drawings in a 17-minute color film; the film emphasizes the contribution of the canal to the growth of America. Bailey Film Associates.

Evans, S. H. *The United States Coast Guard, 1790–1915, A Definitive History*. Annapolis, Maryland: U.S. Naval Institute, 1949. The definitive account of a subject previously ignored, the U.S. Coast Guard. It was in 1915 that the Revenue Cutter Service and the Lifesaving Service merged to become the Coast Guard.

Feth, S. H. *Water Facts and Figures for Planners and Managers*. Washington, D.C.: U.S. Geological Survey, 1973. A sophisticated essay on water in the urban environment, containing charts, a glossary of terms and a bibliography most useful for advanced students and teachers.

Fruchtman, Theodore. *Illustrated Ship's Dictionary: A Handy Compendium of the Most Commonly Used Terms*. New York: Reporter Publications, 1951. A good reference source for commonly used maritime terms.

Great Lakes Ports of North America, The. Ann Arbor, Michigan: The Lesstrang Publishing Corporation. A well-illustrated book on the 22 deepwater ports that lie within the Great Lakes and the St. Lawrence Seaway. The aerial photographs and the information on the ports make this a useful book.

Groenen, L. *Illustrated Marine Encyclopedia*, Toronto: George J. McLeod, Ltd., 1948. Although a good reference work, it is somewhat dated.

Harbor Pilot. BFA Educational Media. The experience of the harbor pilot is portrayed in this 10-minute color film which shows how the skills of the pilot enable him to safely guide ships to port. Bailey Film Associates.

Harding, L. A. *Brief History of the Art of Navigation*. New York: William-Frederick Press, 1952. An analysis of the development of navigation through the ages.

Heritage and Horizons. Washington, D.C.: Department of the Navy. Recently (1976) produced and extremely well-done film. Combines recent naval activity with excellent historical footage.

Historically Famous Lighthouses. Washington, D.C.: U.S. Coast Guard Public Information Division (CG-232). An 88-page booklet containing information on lighthouses located in the coastal and Great Lakes states as well as in Hawaii. The booklet contains a picture and short history of each of the lighthouses. As lighthouses form a romantic and interesting part of our nation's maritime heritage, this booklet provides a useful and enjoyable account of part of our background.

Hohman, E. P. *History of American Merchant Seaman.* Hamden, Connecticut: Shoe String Press, 1956. While less comprehensive than the title indicates, this work provides a good background of the development of the most important maritime trades.

How Ships Are Built. Chester, Pennsylvania: Sun Shipbuilding and Dry Dock Company. A well-done short booklet (with step-by-step photographs) on the building of modern ships. This nontechnical account contains a glossary of ship and marine terms as well as information on types of ships, propulsion, and navigation.

Huntress, Keith. *Narratives of Shipwrecks and Disasters.* Ames, Iowa: Iowa State University Press, 1974. This work covers the 275 years (1586–1860) when wood sailing ships were in their Golden Age. Specifically, the author relates the stories behind the destruction of 24 ships.

Inches, H. C. *The Great Lakes Wooden Shipbuilding Era.* Vermilion, Ohio: Great Lakes Historical Society, 1962. An account particularly useful to teachers in the upper Middle West who wish to integrate some local maritime history into their courses.

Inland Waterborne Commerce Statistics (annually). Washington, D.C.: The American Waterways Operators, Inc. A compilation of the statistics of the commodities carried over the inland waterways such as the Sacramento River and Illinois waterways. It is a valuable and useful reference.

Ives, B. *Sea Songs of Sailing, Whaling and Fishing.* 1956. A good sampling of songs (68) from the sea. Accompanying the words of each song are the melody and guitar chords.

Inland Waterways—Inland Ports. Arthur Barr Productions, P.O. Box 7-C, Pasadena, California 91104. This 15-minute film depicts the importance of water transportation. The film shows a large seagoing freighter's journey upriver to an inland port to deposit its cargo. The port activities (exchange of goods—barges, trains, trucks, ships) are shown.

Jane's Fighting Ships. An annual similar to Brassey's but with more emphasis on details and diagrams. Published since 1898, it contains information on all the navies of the world.

Jobé, Joseph. *The Great Age of Sail.* New York: Time-Life, 1967. A nicely illustrated and well-written popular account of the days when sail was king of the seas.

Johnson, David. *Clipper Ships and the Cutty Sark.* New York: Grossman Publishers, 1971. This collection of primary sources, sketches and narrative accounts of the clipper ships is part of the Jackdaw Series. It is useful in discovery-inquiry lessons or just for posting on bulletin boards.

Kaufman, Betsy B. "The Planning of Multimedia Study: Man's Interest and Fascination with the Sea," *Journal of English Teaching Effectiveness,*

1973. This article is useful to the teacher wishing to approach maritime studies in an interdisciplinary manner. The author lists several valuable books (fiction, nonfiction) for use with students.

Kennedy, Ludovic. *Pursuit.* New York: Pinnacle Books, 1975. A scholarly and very readable account of the chase and sinking of the *Bismarck.* This analysis benefits from material only recently made available (1973) and from a conveying of the drama of the chase.

Kimmel, H. E. *Admiral Kimmel's Story.* Toronto: S. S. Reginald Sanders & Co., Ltd., 1954. Kimmel, naval commander at Pearl Harbor, defends his actions prior to the attack by the Japanese.

Knight, F. E. *The Sea Story, Being a Guide to Nautical Reading from Ancient Times to the Close of the Sailing Ship Era.* London: Macmillan, 1958. A valuable guide to fiction. The author, a retired British ship captain, suggests readings in various categories.

Laing, Alexander. *American Heritage History of Seafaring America.* New York: McGraw-Hill Book Co., 1974. Well-written, superbly illustrated account of the maritime development of the nation. A must selection.

Life in an Eastern Seaport Town 1870. ACI Media, 35 West 45th Street, New York, N.Y. 10017. Although somewhat narrative, this film contains an abundance of information on life in a whaling town; filmed in Mystic, Nantucket and New York, the photography enhances the production.

Lewis, C. L. *Books of the Sea, An Introduction to Nautical Literature.* Westport, Connecticut; Greenwood Press, Inc., 1943. Includes both critical reviews and listings of works, novels, short stories, poetry, plays. Examples of chapters: Naval History, Ships and Merchant Marine, Biographies of Seamen, Pirates, Mutineers and Slavers.

Lloyd, Christopher. *Ships and Seamen: From the Vikings to the Present Day, A History in Text and Pictures.* Cleveland: World Publication, 1961. The author has pulled together a fine collection of pictures to complement his text.

Lord, W. *A Night To Remember.* New York: Holt, Rinehart and Winston, Inc., 1955. This book describes the sinking of the great White Star liner *Titanic* on April 15, 1912, with the loss of 1198 lives.

Lott, Arnold and Eloise Engle. *America's Maritime Heritage.* Annapolis, Maryland: U.S. Naval Institute, 1975. A high school textbook, the first of its kind, is directed at students in the NROTC program. Lavishly illustrated, it provides a host of information on many maritime subjects for teacher and student.

Lovette, L. P. *Naval Customs, Traditions and Usage.* Annapolis, Maryland: U.S. Naval Institute, 1959. This publication exists as a useful handbook for the student or teacher with questions about naval terminology and traditions.

MacDonald, R. N. *Using Tools—Whaling.* Cambridge, Massachusetts: Educational Development Center, Inc., 1974. A unit in the curriculum project "People and Technology" focusing on a case study investigation of a highly developed craft technology. The experimental unit contains many types of good instructional materials and media (a film, filmstrips, a simulation game, artifacts, primary sources, a poster, and a model ship construction kit). The unit contains the ingredients for interesting interdisciplinary student-oriented lessons based upon whaling life in early Nantucket.

McClung, Robert. *Treasures in the Sea.* Washington, D.C.: National Geographic Society, 1972. Colorfully illustrated with pictures, maps and reproductions of paintings, this short book, part of the Books for Young Explorers Series, is an excellent choice for primary and middle school students.

McCosker, M. S. *The Historical Collection of Insurance Company of North America.* Philadelphia: Insurance Company of North America, 1967. This book contains an annotated list of marine paintings, prints, books, records, ship models and other memorabilia contained in the company's collection, which is located in libraries around the country. In addition, the book contains many beautiful illustrations of the above.

McFee, William. *The Law of the Sea.* Philadelphia: Lippincott, 1950. The author has written a summary of the historical development of maritime law.

Manning, G. C. *The Theory and Technique of Ship Design: A Study of the Basic Principles and Processes Employed in the Design of Ships of All Classes.* Cambridge, Mass.: Massachusetts Institute of Technology, 1956. The author, a professor at M.I.T., provides the reader with useful information as to the basics of ship design.

"Meet the Press—Admiral E. R. Zumwalt, Jr." Sunday, June 30, 1974. An in-depth interview in which Zumwalt talks about the present state of the Navy and makes predictions for the future. Zumwalt also discusses innovations he introduced into the Navy while he served as Chief of Naval Operations. (Merkle Press, Washington, D.C.).

"Merchant Marine"—Merchant Marine, Officers, Merchant Seamen. Reprint from *Occupational Outlook Handbook,* (1975–75 Edition) Bulletin 1785–140. A good source of information for career education advisement; it contains information on qualifications, salary and opportunities.

Merrill, J. M. *Quarterdeck and Fo'c'sle; The exciting story of the Navy.* Chicago: Rand McNally, 1963. A collection of primary sources (reports, logs, letters) from the Revolution to the present. Excellent for use with students in present or abbreviated form.

Meyers, Judith. *Waldo the Whale.* Mystic, Conn.: Education Department, Marine Historical Association. A short booklet designed for upper elementary school students, it deals with whaling in an educational and humanistic fashion. The educational department of the Marine Historical Association is one of the few organizations producing educational materials in this field.

Mississippi River Navigation. Vicksburg, Mississippi: Mississippi River Commission, 1971. A booklet containing a significant amount of information about the river. In addition to a history of the river, maps, charts and pictures are included.

Morison, S. E. *Maritime History of Massachusetts, 1783–1860,* 1921. This work provides insight into the early development of American trade, shipbuilding, and the fishing industry. Also valuable because of Morison's fine writing ability and his prominence as the nation's leading maritime historian.

"Naval and Maritime Prize Photography" Contest Winners. U.S. Naval Institute Annapolis, Maryland 21402. A reprint booklet of photographs that have won the annual contest sponsored by the U.S. Naval Institute. Photographs (color and black-and-white) are of frameable quality. The

Institute also is a prime source of photographs of ships; it has a collection of several thousand pictures.

Navy, Marine Corps and Coast Guard. Washington, D.C.: Government Printing Office. A listing of government publications relating to the Navy, Marines and Coast Guard. These publications include topics such as safety, military law, astronomy, radar and oceanography.

Neuhaus, H. M. "Fifty Years of Naval Engineering." *American Society of Naval Engineers Journal.* V. 50, 1938. This four-part article covers the development of naval engineering from 1888 to 1938.

"*Old Navy I, II Portfolio.*" The National Archives, Washington, D.C. 20408. These outstanding prints from the Franklin D. Roosevelt collection, reproduced in color on quality paper at a reasonable cost (20 prints, $3.50), can be used for school displays and classroom bulletin boards.

O'Neill, Eugene. *The Complete Works of Eugene O'Neill.* New York: Random House. This collection contains many plays with a maritime setting (aboard a barge, a trans-Atlantic liner, a merchant ship) and maritime themes (death at sea, loneliness, frontier). O'Neill, one of America's great playwrights, chose the sea as the setting for many of his plays.

Operation Rescue—Cleaning and Care of Oiled Waterfowl. Washington, D.C.: American Petroleum Institute. A booklet written in response to criticism of oil spills and their effects, this publication tells of the development of techniques to treat birds that have come in contact with oil. The booklet is interesting not only for its treatment of this topic but also for its material on water pollution (by oil) in general.

Port of Duluth-Superior. Duluth, Minn.: Seaway Port Authority. This is a short, illustrated booklet dealing with the ports of Duluth and Superior. Duluth, as the nation's number 2 port (in tonnage), deserves the attention of the student of American studies and maritime affairs. All major ports and most minor ports have such publications available free.

Potter, E. B. and C. W. Nimitz. *Sea Power: A Naval History.* Englewood Cliffs, N.J.: Prentice Hall, 1960. This volume, a history of the American Navy, is the text used at Annapolis and in NROTC programs.

Recreation. District Corps of Engineers, Department of the Army. A booklet illustrated lavishly with pictures and maps of American recreational waterways. Information on each facility includes availability of water skiing, pools, swimming, etc.

Robinson, S. S. and M. Robinson. *A History of Naval Tactics from 1530 to 1930.* Annapolis, Maryland: U.S. Naval Institute, 1942. An in-depth treatment of the development of naval strategy over four centuries. The authors cover many battles and wars including those in which the United States was not involved.

Rodgers, W. L. *Naval Warfare Under Oars—14th to 16th Centuries.* Annapolis, Maryland: U.S. Naval Institute, 1940. A comprehensive, well-illustrated study of naval warfare, strategy and tactics from the time of the Roman Empire to the Spanish Armada.

Selected Oceanographic Publications. Washington, D.C.: U.S. Government Printing Office. A short annotated bibliography of publications available from the U.S. Government Printing Office. These publications are generally short essays and booklets.

Shipping World Year Book, The. An annual containing directories of shipowners, statistical information, maritime rules and regulations, and shipping organizations. Published since 1887, it is a very useful handbook of yearly maritime activities.

Snell, Tee Loftin. *The Wild Shores—America's Beginnings.* Washington, D.C.: National Geographic Society, 1974. A well-written historical analysis of early American life along the coast, liberally illustrated with excellent pictures and sketches.

Songs and Sounds of the Sea. Washington, D.C.: National Geographic Society, 1973. (Stereo-record) A collection of American folk songs related to the sea. These songs, mingled with the sounds of the sea, are heard as they were sung by the hardy men who are so much a part of America's maritime tradition.

Spectorsky, A. C. (Ed.) *The Book of the Sea.* New York: Appleton, 1954. This is an anthology containing 83 well-chosen selections. This massive work of 488 pages contains many excellent illustrations.

Stackpole, E. A. *The Sea Hunters.* Toronto: Lippincott, 1953. Stackpole's account of early America exists as the most authoritative publication of the topic.

Starbuck, A. A. *A History of the Whaling Industry . . . to the Year 1876.* Old Dartmouth Historical Society, 1959. R. B. Hegarty and P. F. Purrington continued the book until 1928.

Steamboat Bill. BFA Educational Media. The film relates the tale of the famous riverboat captain, beginning with Bill's days in Council Bluff, Iowa, when he was determined to become "the most famous riverboat captain." This 11-minute color film portrays the lure of the river.

Theobald, R. A. *The Final Secret of Pearl Harbor: The Washington Contribution to the Japanese Attack.* New York: Devin-Adair, 1954. Theobald, a Navy admiral, defends Admiral Kimmel, asserting that President Roosevelt and his advisors provoked the attack.

Those in Peril on the Sea. This work contains first-person narrative accounts of battles against the sea by 18 survivors.

"Treasure Maps and Charts." *Social Education,* Vol. 35, No. 1, December, 1971. An annotated bibliography of treasure maps and charts listing locations of sunken ships. The bibliography lists addresses for obtaining the maps.

Villiers, Captain A. *Men, Ships and the Sea.* Washington, D.C.: National Geographic Society, 1972 (new edition). This is clearly one of the outstanding pictorial and narrative accounts of the historical development of ships. It contains chapters such as "Medieval Marines Enrich Coasts with Commerce," "Yankee Merchants Tap China Trade," "Steamboats a-Comin'!," "Dreadnoughts and Blue Riband Liners" and "Small Boating: Everybody's Sport."

Waller, George. *Pearl Harbor: Roosevelt and the Coming of the War.* Boston: D. C. Heath, 1965. One of the books in the D. C. Heath "Problems in American Civilization" series. Several authors provide conflicting analyses of the reasons for Pearl Harbor.

Wescott, A. (Ed.) *Mahan on Naval Warfare: Selections from the Writings of Rear Admiral T. Mahan.* A collection of the most significant passages from the works of Mahan, who formulated the "sea power" theory. Prior to his death in 1917, Mahan had written 20 books and approximately 100 articles.

Wilkes, C. *Narrative of the Exploring Expedition, 1838–42.* The first major exploring expedition undertaken by the U.S. Navy under the command of Charles Wilkes, U.S.N. The expedition contributed to the advancement of knowledge in many disciplines (meteorology, anthropology) and scored a first in proving the existence of the continent of Antartica.

Wise, Donald A. *A Descriptive List of Treasure Maps and Charts in the Library of Congress.* Washington, D.C.: U.S. Government Printing Office, 1973. This recent revision lists the general location of sunken treasure ships off both coasts.

Wohlstetter, Roberta. *Pearl Harbor: Warning and Decision.* Stanford, California: Stanford University Press, 1962. A scholarly, systematic, though not very readable account (heavy in primary sources) of the attack upon Pearl Harbor. Wohlstetter emphasizes the poor coordination of communication between the Army, Navy and the Government.

United States Merchant Marine—A Brief History. Washington, D.C.: U.S. Department of Commerce Maritime Administration, 1972. A short (seven pages) booklet explaining the history of the Merchant Marine and its role and importance in the country's development. A well-written, concise essay with illustrations.

United States Naval History: A Bibliography. Washington, D.C.: Naval History Division Department of the Navy, 1972. This is an extensive bibliography of writings (reports, books, pamphlets, articles) on the Navy and all its activities (armament, strategy, tactics, history, periodicals, research aids, etc.).

"United States Navy Lithographs." Washington, D.C.: Government Printing Office. These six sets deal with notable highlights and battles, the evolution of officers' and enlisted men's uniforms, and recruiting posters. Relatively inexpensive, they are suitable for bulletin board use or framing.

United States Submarine Data Book. Groton, Connecticut: Submarine Force Library and Museum. A booklet on each of America's submarines—type of design, displacement, first commissioning, shipyard, length, disposition, etc. Groton, home of U.S. Naval Submarine Base (New London) is considered "submarine capital of the world."

Naval and Maritime Museums

The following is a list of the locations of museums that can provide valuable field trip learning experiences for teachers and students. Individual museums should be contacted for brochures describing holdings and procedures. (Modified from *U.S. Naval Institute Proceedings* [October, 1966] and *Marine Museums in the United States*. This is an abridged listing.)

Alabama

Dauphin Island: Fort Gaines Museum, USS *Hartford*
Mobile: USS *Alabama*, USS *Drum*, USS *Tecumseh*.

Alaska

Juneau: Relics of USS *Juneau*.

California

China Lake: Michelson Museum, Naval Ordnance Test Station.
Long Beach: SS *Queen Mary*.
Los Angeles: California Museum of Science and Industry, 700 State Drive.
Port Hueneme: Seabee Museum.
San Diego: Naval Training Center Historical Museum, Building 30; Ship *Star of India;* Maritime Museum of San Diego.
San Francisco: San Francisco Maritime Museum, San Francisco Maritime State Historical Monument, Schooner C. A. *Thayer*, Steam-Schooner *Wapama*, Scow Schooner *Alma*, Ferry *Eureka*, 2905 Hyde Street; Sloop *Gjoa*, Golden Gate Park; Spreckles Museum, Treasure Island.
San Pedro: Cabrillo Marine Museum.
Vallejo: Mare Island Naval Shipyard Museum.

Connecticut

Groton: Midget submarine type *Seehund II, HU-75;* two Japanese midget submarines, U.S. Naval Submarine Base; The Submarine Library, U.S. Naval Submarine Base.
Hartford: Marine Room, Wadsworth Athenaeum
Mystic: Marine Historical Association and Mystic Seaport, Whaleship *Charles W. Morgan*, Ship *Joseph Conrad*, Schooner *L. A. Dunton*, Sandbagger *Annie*, Cutter *Fox*, Sloop *Estella A.*, Schooner *Bowdoin, Dorothy Parsons, Regina M.*, Schooner *Pleione, Gundel*.
New London: U.S. Coast Guard Museum, *Eagle* cutter and training ship, USS *Flasher*.

District of Columbia

Santa Maria, Maine Avenue; Smithsonian Institution, Constitution Avenue; Truxtun-Decatur Naval Museum, 1610 H Street, N.W.; U.S. Naval Historical Display Center, Washington Navy Yards; Washington National Archives, Pennsylvania Avenue at 8th Street, N.W.; USS *Gyatt*, USS *Torsk*, *Intelligent Whale* (Civil War submarines).

Florida

Fort Lauderdale: *Golden Doubloon*, SS *Queen Elizabeth*.
Marathon: Sunken Treasure Ship Museum.
Pensacola: Naval Aviation Museum, U.S. Naval Air Station.
St. Petersburg: HMS *Bounty* (restoration).

Georgia

Columbus: Confederate Naval Museum; CSS *Muscogee*, CSS *Chattahoochee*.
Savannah: Model of SS *Savannah* at City Hall; Ships of the Sea Museum, *Flying Cloud* (eight foot model), *Harbor Queen*.

Hawaii

Honolulu: Bernice P. Bishop Museum, *Falls of Clyde*.
Pearl Harbor: USS *Arizona* Memorial; USS *Utah*; Japanese midget submarine; USS *Bowfin*.

Illinois

Chicago: Chicago Historical Society, Clark Street and North Avenue; George F. Harding Museum, Randolph and Michigan Avenue; Museum of Science and Industry, Submarine *U-505* (German, World War II), 57th Street and Lake Shore Drive; Replica of Viking ship in Lincoln Park.
East St. Louis: USS *Cero*.
Lockport: Illinois and Michigan Canal Museum.

Indiana

Bloomington: Mainmast and guns of USS *Indiana*.
Jeffersonville: Howard National Steamboat Museum.

Iowa

Clinton: *Showboat*.
Keokuk: Keokuk River Museum on board *George M. Verity*.

Kentucky

Louisville: *Belle of Louisville*.

Louisiana

Baton Rouge: CSS *Arkansas.*
New Orleans: CSS *Pioneer;* Louisiana State Museum.

Maine

Bath: Bath Marine Museum; Percy and Small Shipyard.
Booth Bay Harbor: *Sherman Zwicker; Sequin.*
Camden: USS *Bowdoin.*
Castine: Maine Maritime Museum.
Portland: Maine Historical Society, Cape Elizabeth Lighthouse (1828).
Searsport: Penobscot Marine Museum.

Maryland

Annapolis: Historic Annapolis, Inc., Slicer Shiplap House, 18 Pinkney
   Street; U.S. Naval Academy Museum; U.S. Naval Acade.ny Library.
Baltimore: Maryland Historical Society, Marine Wing, 201 W. Monument
   Street; USS *Constellation;* The Steamship Historical Society of America
   Library.
Landover Hills: Nautical Research Guild.
Piney Point: *Dauntless,* Harry Lundeberg School of Seamanship.
St. Michaels: Chesapeake Bay Maritime Museum, *J. T. Leonard, Barnegat*
   Lightship.

Massachusetts

Andover: Addison Gallery of American Art, Phillips Academy.
Barnstable: The Donald G. Trayser Memorial Museum.
Boston: Boston Marine Society; Museum of Fine Arts; Old State House;
   Museum of Science, Science Park; State Street Trust Company; Stebbins
   Marine Collection, Harrison Grey Otis House; USS *Constitution,* Boston
   Naval Shipyard.
Cambridge: Francis Russell Hart Nautical Museum, Massachusetts In-
   stitute of Technology, 77 Massachusetts Avenue.
Chatham: Whaling Museum.
Cohasset: Maritime Museum.
Edgartown: Dukes County Historical Society, Martha's Vineyard.
Fall River: Fall River Historical Society Museum; USS *Massachusetts,* State
   Pier, USS *Lionship.*
Gloucester: Gloucester Art Institute.
Mattapoisett: Mattapoisett Historical Society.
Nantucket: Nantucket Whaling Museum, Pete Foulger Museum.
Nantucket Island: Nantucket Historical Association.
Milton: Museum of the American China Trade.
New Bedford: Whaling Museum and Old Dartmouth Historical Society.
Newburyport: Newburyport Historical Society.

Plymouth: *Mayflower II* (replica of original *Mayflower*).
Salem: Peabody Museum, 161 Essex Street; Salem Maritime National His-
  toric Sites, Custom House, 168 Derby Street, and Derby House, 172
  Derby Street; Essex Institute, Essex Street.
Sharon: Kendall Whaling Museum.

Michigan

Dearborn: Greenfield Village, Steamer *Swanee*.
Detroit: Detroit Historical Society; Dossin Museum of Great Lakes History,
  Belle Isle.
Menominee: Mystery Ship Seaport.
Sault Ste. Marie: Museum Ship *Valley Camp*, Great Lakes freighter.

Minnesota

Winona: Transportation Museum on board the *Julius C. Wilkie*.

Mississippi

Biloxi: USS *Biloxi*.
Vicksburg: Mississippi River Museum and Hall of Fame on board the
  Steamer *Sprague;* USS *Cairo*.

Missouri

Hannibal: Steamer *Mark Twain*.
Hermann: Historic Hermann Museum, including Riverboat Room.
St. Louis: Missouri Historical Society, River Room, Lindell at De Baliviere
  Streets; *Golden Rod;* USS *Inaugural*.

Nebraska

Wahoo: Memorial to USS *Wahoo*.

New Hampshire

Portsmouth: Portsmouth Athenaeum, Library, paintings, ship models.

New Jersey

Barnegat Light: Historical Society Museum, typical of many of the mu-
  seums located along the New Jersey coast.
Paterson: City of Paterson Museum; *Fenian Ram*.
Sandyhook: Sandyhook Lighthouse.

New York

Amagansett: Town Marine Museum.
Brooklyn: Brooklyn Museum.
Buffalo: Buffalo & Erie County Historical Society.

Clayton: Thousand Islands Shipyard Museum.
Cold Spring Harbor, L.I.: Whaling Museum.
East Hampton: East Hampton Town Marine Museum.
Glen Cove, L.I.: Webb Institute of Naval Architecture.
Huntington, L.I.: Vanderbilt Marine Museum.
Hyde Park: Franklin D. Roosevelt Library and Museum.
Lake Champlain: Fort Ticonderoga Museum.
New York City: India House, Hanover Square; Metropolitan Museum of Art; Museum of Science and Industry, Marine Transportation Section, Rockefeller Center; Museum of the City of New York, Maritime Museum, 1220 Fifth Avenue; New York Historical Society, 170 Central Park West at 77th Street; Seamen's Bank for Savings, 30 Wall Street; Seamen's Church Institute, 25 South Street; New York Public Library, Fifth Avenue at 42nd Street; New York Public Library, St. George Branch, Staten Island; New York Yacht Club, 37 West 44th Street; Steamship Historical Society of America, 4 Broad Street; South Street Seaport, *Ambrose Lightship, Lettie G. Howard, Alexander Hamilton, Moshulu.*
Sag Harbor: Suffolk County Whaling Museum.
Staten Island: Staten Island Museum; The Steamship Historical Society of America Library.
Syracuse: The Canal Museum.
West Brighton, Staten Island: Sailor's Snug Harbor.
Whitehall: Skenesborough Museum; USS *Ticonderoga.*

North Carolina

Beaufort: Alphonso Whaling Museum.
Kingston: CSS *Neuse*, Governor Richard Caswell Memorial.
Wilmington: USS *North Carolina.*

Ohio

Canal Fulton: Old Canal Days Museum; *St. Helena II.*
Cleveland: Great Lakes Historical Society.
Fairport Harbor: Fairport Marine Museum.
Marietta: Rivermen's Museum; Steamboat *W. P. Snyder.*
Vermillion: Great Lakes Historical Society Museum, 142 Main Street.

Oklahoma

Catoosa: USS *Sea Dog.*

Oregon

Astoria: Columbia River Maritime Museum.
Hood River: USS *Banning.*
Newport: Old Yacquina Bay Lighthouse (1871).

Pennsylvania

Doylestown: Marine Room, Bucks County Historical Society.
Erie: USS *Niagara*.
Philadelphia: Franklin Institute; Philadelphia Maritime Museum, 427 Chestnut Street; Atwater Kent Museum, 15 South 7th Street; Insurance Company of North America Museum, 1600 Arch Street; USS *Olympia; Welcome* (replica of William Penn's ship).

Rhode Island

Bristol: Herreshoff Model Room.
East Greenwich: Varnum Military and Naval Museum.
Newport: New England Naval and Maritime Museum; Newport Historical Society, USS *Constellation*, HMS *Rose*.
Providence: Rhode Island Historical Society.

South Carolina

Charleston: USS *Maine;* Patriot's Point Maritime and Naval Museum, USS *Yorktown*.

South Dakota

Sioux Falls: USS *South Dakota* Memorial Museum.

Tennessee

Jacksonville: USS *Key West*, USS *Tawah*, USS *Elfin* (restoration planned).

Texas

Fredericksburg: Fleet Admiral Chester W. Nimitz Naval Museum.
San Jacinto: USS *Texas;* USS *Cabrilla;* USS *Seawolf* Memorial.

Utah

Clearfield: USS *Utah Bell*.
Salt Lake City: USS *Indiana* armor plate at Medical Center.

Vermont

Shelburne: Shelburne Museum, Steamer *Ticonderoga*.

Virginia

Jamestown: *Discovery, Goodspeed,* and *Susan Constant*.
Newport News: The Mariners Museum.
Norfolk: USS Franklin (bridge of ship), SS *United States*.
Portsmouth: Norfolk Naval Shipyard Museum; Portsmouth Coast Guard Museum, Inc.; *Portsmouth* (lightship).

Virginia Beach: Cape Henry Lighthouse (1792).
Yorktown: Colonial National Park Museum.

Washington

Bremerton: Puget Sound Naval Shipyard Museum, USS *Missouri*.
Seattle: The Museum of History and Industry; Joshua Green-Dwight Merrill Maritime Wing; McCurdy Park; Schooner *Wawona*.

West Virginia

Clarksburg: USS *West Virginia*, flagstaff.
Morgantown: USS *West Virginia*, mast.

Wisconsin

Manitowoc: USS *Red Fin*.

6. Minicourse 2: "Sports Literature"

Introduction

In any minicourse with strong emphasis upon reading, the instructor must be keenly sensitive to the time factor in view of the heterogeneous nature of the students. The one-week course may have as reading requirements some short pieces from an anthology or a short paperback; whereas, the lengthier course permits exploration of more readings and diverse topics. In a course dealing with sports literature it is hoped that, in addition to the primary objectives related to the literature, additional goals be related to basic process skills. Reading, writing, and speaking seem easily related to the subject. Planning must also include time to develop these objectives. A lesson could revolve around a sports journalism writing experience. Showing several times parts of a film (or videotape) of an athletic event can serve as a springboard into an assignment, such as, "Imagine yourself as a sportswriter—write a 250-word article on the sports event you are about to view." Assignments like this can challenge all students to their best performance.

If time permits, the teacher should also try to integrate into the course differentiated assignments—that is, there will be some items read by all students, then a list from which students can make additional selections. Frequently, the latter serves as the basis for individual or group talks to class.

The following is an outline of the structure of sports literature in its most generic sense!

CATEGORIES OF SPORTS LITERATURE

    I. Fiction (and Poetry)
   II. Technical
      a. for the fan
      b. for the player
      c. for the coach
  III. General Interest
  IV. Biography and Autobiography
   V. Anthologies
  VI. Newspapers
 VII. Magazines
VIII. Nonprint Media
  IX. Bulletin Board Materials
   X. Exposé and Protest

On examining its structure, it becomes quickly apparent that sports literature exists as one of the most diverse fields within literature. Furthermore, the number of works in the field guarantees something for everyone. The nation's sport mania has expanded beyond the traditional sports (football, basketball, baseball) to a noticeable growth of minor sports (soccer, lacrosse), lifetime sports (tennis, golf), and women's sports. Whether sports participant or sports fan, the student can find in a minicourse like this opportunities to grow in many ways. This is particularly important in stimulating the reluctant reader.

The following are explanations of each of the categories with illustrative examples for clarification.

Fiction

Several fiction stories exist that are well written, readable, and inspirational for young people; they are available both in hardbound and paperback. There have been, however, some criticisms of this field. Consider the following:

> If there is one fault common to most sport stories, it is the formula plot: the beginner, from school playground to professional team, who can't get along with another member of the team or the coach because he is cocky, or because he wants things his own way, eventually rises to heights of glory and acceptance by all because he saves the final game in the last minute of play. Another fault common to such stories is the thin plot wrapped around long and often tedious game sequences.[1]

The above critique is obviously an extreme simplification and certainly true of only part of the field. More importantly, the central theme of the hero overcoming adversity and achieving success is one that young people can clearly identify with, and it is this theme that makes sports literature so valuable. Sports fiction is such a widely diverse field that teachers will easily be able to provide the appropriate themes for the student. Works such as Henry G. Felsen's *Hot Rod* (Bantam), Fred Bachman's *Hang In at the Plate* (Walch), Marguerite Henry's *King of the Wind* (Rand McNally), E. L. Konigsburg's *About the B'nai Bagels* (Atheneum), and Robert Lipsyte's *The Contender* (Bantam) are just a sample of what is available.

Technical

Technical works vary in their level of complexity and, accordingly, in their utility. In this category, relatively few simplified texts are available for the fan. However, most general interest books that deal with a particular team or player will contain some references and explanations of the team's successful offensive and defensive strategies or a player's philosophy toward an aspect of the game, such as, hitting in baseball (Mickey Mantle's *The Education of a Baseball Player*, Simon and Schuster) or training in swimming (Don Schollander and Michael Savage's *Deep Water*, Crown). Clair Bee's *Basketball for Everyone* (Ace Books) devotes a substantial portion of the book to "Spectator: Know Your Basketball" providing technical information on "How to Watch the Game," "Styles of Offense," and "Defense-Different Types." "Red" Auerbach's *Basketball for the Player, the Fan and the Coach* (Simon and Schuster) is also a good selection.

Clary Anderson's *Make the Team in Basketball* (Grosset and Dunlap), Jim Leighton's *Inside Tennis: Techniques of Winning* (Prentice-Hall), Bill Gottlieb's *Table Tennis* (Knopf) and Skip O'Connor's *How to Star in Track and Field* (Four Winds) and *Baseball Rules in Pictures* by Jacobs and McCrory (Grosset and Dunlap) exist as examples of the how-to-do-it volumes available to serve the needs of the athlete or aspiring athlete. Most of these—characterized by sketches and pictures demonstrating correct positioning, stance, and technique—are well written. A note of caution should be sounded with regard to two things: (1) Dated books may present certain techniques or aspects of playing that are outmoded or no longer permitted because of rule changes. While the essence of each sport remains the same, changes in emphasis may make chapters of certain books not as valuable as others. (2) The importance of the fundamentals of the game—passing, sliding, blocking—cannot be underemphasized. When making selections in this category, books should contain a chapter or chapters on developing the fundamental skills so important to the success of athletes.

While the majority of technical coaching books are above the level of students, some players are mature enough to benefit from such materials. Works in this area could generally serve the teacher/coach offering a course in "Sports Appreciation," "Athletic Coaching Strategies" or "How to Watch Athletic Contests." Examples of books in this category are Jack Ramsey's *Pressure Defense* (Prentice-Hall) and Dale Froster's *Slanting Monster Defense in Football* (Parker Publishing). "Leg Wrestling Series" (*Beacon Falls Coaches Digest*, 1968–69) "Water Polo Weight Training" (*Swimming World*, October, 1970), "Training for the Mile" (*Athletic Journal*, February, 1971), "Improving Your Overhead Smash (in Tennis)" (*Coach and Athlete*, April, 1974) and "The Confidence Game" (Janie Blalock, *Sportswoman*, March–April, 1976) are examples of selected articles that teachers may wish to have students read. Articles can provide excellent supplementary readings to paperbacks in this area.

General Interest

Many outstanding sports books fall into the general interest category. Frequently authored by journalists, these well-written, well-illustrated texts can be subclassified into circulating and noncirculating reference works. John Arlott's *Oxford Companion to World Sports and Games* (Oxford), Dick Schaap's *Illustrated History of the Olympics* (Knopf), Henry Walker's *Illustrated Baseball Dictionary for Young People* (Harvey House), Milton Shapiro's *A Treasury of Sports Humor* (Messner), John Durant's *The Sports of Our Presidents* (Macmillan), Herbert Kamm's *The New Senior Illustrated Encyclopedia of Sports*, Norris and Ross McWhiter's *Guiness Sports Record Book* (Sterling) and the multi-volume *Lincoln Library of Sports Champions* (Frontier) are examples of outstanding general interest reference works the teachers may wish to display for short reading and reference examination. Any course in this classification will surely result in the necessity for teachers and students to research sports trivia. Others in this classification need more study by the reader and fall into the circulating collection classification—Howard Liss' *Champions of the Little League*

(Messner), Al Hall's *Complete Guide to the Bicycle* (Peterson), Robert Peterson's *Only the Ball Was White* (Prentice-Hall), Bobby Riggs' *Court Hustler* (Lippincott), Sir Edmund Hillary's *Nothing Venture, Nothing Win* (Coward, McCann and Geoghegan), Mac Davis' *Strange and Incredible Sports Happenings* (Grosset and Dunlap), George Barr's *Here's Why: Science in Sports* (Scholastic) and Lee Arthur's *Sports Math* (Lothrop).

Biographies and Autobiographies

Biographies and autobiographies have long interested both the school athlete and the curious, and constitute a large percentage of publications classified as sports literature. Most young people, because they are impressionable, are interested in contemporary heroes—Beth Wilson's *Muhammed Ali* (Putnam), Linda Jacob's *Annemarie Proell: Queen of the Mountain* (EMC), John Devaney's *Tom Seaver* (Popular Library), Bernie Young's *Picture Story of Frank Robinson* (Messner), Robert Jackson's *Earl and Pearl: The Story of Baltimore's Earl Monroe* (Walck), and Dave Wolf's *Foul! Connie Hawkins, School Yard Star, Exile NBA Superstar* (Holt, Rinehart and Winston). Still, the sports immortals should not be ignored—Alice Thorne's *Clemente* (Grosset and Dunlap), Babe Ruth and Bob Considine's *The Babe Ruth Story* (Scholastic), Jesse Owens and Paul Heimark's *Black Think* (Morrow), and Althea Gibson's (and Edward Fitzgerald) *I Always Wanted to Be Somebody* (Harper and Row). Books in this category have been supplemented recently by multimedia biographies such as the *Women Who Win* series (EMC) in which a tape cassette of the book accompanies the book. These books can be extremely beneficial for the beginning and intermediate reader and for the English-as-a-second-language student. This category, because of interest in athletes and the high quality of writing (most are written by journalists or athletes in combination with journalists) has been well received by students and should receive serious consideration in selection of instructional materials.

Anthologies

Sports anthologies provide reading for young people in the categories of both fact and fiction and can be used totally or partially, depending upon objectives and course length. Arna BonTemp's *Famous Negro Athletes* (Dodd, Mead) has particular value not only as one of the few anthologies devoted to minority group athletes but also for its coverage of minor sports. In Margaret and Edwin Hyde's *Where Speed Is King* (McGraw-Hill) each chapter is devoted to a sport (track, skiing, racing) and the personalities that have broken the speed records in it. Mac Davis' *Baseball's Unforgetables* (Bantam) contains several short, interesting, and unusual stories that will amuse any reader. Steve Gehman's *Young Olympic Champions* (Norton) details some of the young men and women who have attained the gold medal. Devoting a chapter to each champion, the author covers the pre-Olympic athletic developments and achievements of each as well as the successes at the Olympic games; the diversity of the book in covering many sports (track, basketball, skiing), both U.S. and foreign athletes of different races and both sexes make it a particularly fine choice.

Anthologies of short fictional sport stories can provide both the athlete and nonathlete enjoyable and productive reading. Of particular value are Frank Owen's *Teenage Sport Stories* (Latern), *Boy's Life Book of Sports Stories* (Random House) and Don McKay's *Wild Wheels* (Dell). These anthologies can be particularly useful for the slow reader because of the brevity and high interest associated with most sport stories.

Newspapers

A weekly newspaper, *Sporting News*, contains several articles and a wealth of statistics in each issue. Characterized by a large color front-page picture of a player or players in action, this paper contains in each issue a couple of in-depth articles on players and teams of in-season sports. The detailed statistics included constitute an excellent source of information for player and fan. The major sports also have specific newspapers that contain detailed treatments of that sport. For example, *Basketball News and Times*, published weekly, contains articles on coaches, players, teams and developments at the professional, collegiate, and high school level. While most teachers will wish to use a general newspaper like *Sporting News*, some, because of a specific course or because a particular community or school district identifies with a particular sport, may wish to add an additional paper, such as, *Football News*, to their collection. Many of these are available on a seasonal basis.

Magazines

Sports magazines, though somewhat expensive and saturated with advertising, can appeal to almost all readers. They can be

74

divided into two categories—technical, for coaches and advanced players, and general, for the fan and the general public. *Athletic Journal, Scholastic Coach,* and *Coach Athlete* are general technical journals suggested for high school libraries (others in this category—*Coaching Clinic, Basketball Clinic*—are highly technical and too expensive for recommended use). General magazines such as *Sports Illustrated* (with the largest circulation), *Sport, Black Sports,* and local editions such as *Sports Philadelphia* attract the interest of the fan, the athlete and the general public. Seasonal or annual journals (published once a year), *College Football, Pro Basketball,* considering interest and the condition of minicourse program budgets should generally not become part of the collection. In certain geographic areas and schools with a particular attachment to a specific sport, the instructor may wish to acquire a subscription to a journal or magazine such as *Skin Diver, Boating, Swimming World,* and *World Tennis* for use during the course and for availability to students thereafter. Also, some of the traditional standbys, *Hot Rod Magazine* and *Motor Trend Magazine,* can be joined by *Women Sports* and *Sports Woman.* A new magazine designed for libraries and young children, *In Sports,* is now available four times a year in hardback.

Both magazines and newspapers provide good sources of articles that can be used in consort with other instructional materials.

Nonprint Media

The expansion of nonprint materials for classroom instruction has been matched by a concurrent, although not as extensive or dramatic, development in the sports field. Several filmstrips useful to students are available: "Introducing Volleyball" and "Introducing Badmitton" (National Film Board of Canada), "Learn to Swim" (BFA Educational Media) and "How to Play Softball" (Athletic Institute) are typical. Athlete Institute's recently developed (1976) sound filmstrip series with titles such as "Basketball," "Ice Hockey" and "Track" is extremely well done and an excellent selection for the library that serves the elementary and middle school student. Also quite suitable for classroom or for student library usage on an individualized basis are silent film loops: these are both more numerous and more diverse than filmstrips. Typical titles vary from "Basketball: Jump Shot" (Athletic Institute), "Golf: The Putt" (Athletic Institute), "Volleyball: Net Volley" (BFA Educational Media), "Soccer: Dribbling and Running with the Ball" (Encyclopedia Britannica Educational Corporation), "Bowling" (BFA

Educational Media) and "Women's Basketball: Cross-Over Dribble and Reverse Dribble" (Athletic Institute). Several sound film loops are now also available—"Golf: How to Build a Swing," "Soccer: Basic Individual Skills" and "Tennis: Forehand and Backhand Stroke Fundamentals" (Athletic Institute).

The short silent film loops (three to five minutes), the longer sound film loops (generally sixteen to twenty-two minutes) and filmstrips can be interesting and informative for students; the more technical film loops—"Basketball Offense: Triple Post, Shuffle Offense, 1–4 Offense" (BFA Educational Media) are recommended for use in very specialized minicourses ("Coaching Techniques," "How to Watch Basketball") as opposed to the more general courses ("Sports Literature," "Sports Appreciation").

Some recently developed multimedia kits should be given serious consideration for purchase—"Sports Close-Ups" (Brentwood House), "Sports Superstars" (Creative Education), and "Women Who Win" (EMC). Troll's multimedia skill kits (examples are "Karate for Sport and Self-Defense," "Baseball: How to Hit and Run") combine a booklet, filmstrip, cassette, activity cards to form an outstanding multimedia kit that can motivate and promote readings skills. Sports films and movies can be obtained from the usual sources (film libraries, etc.). In addition, many companies producing sports materials offer films as a free service, which indirectly promotes their product. For example, Converse Rubber Company annually makes available "Basketball Highlights," which reviews the previous season. Modern Talking Picture Service and Association-Sterling Films, both located in New York City, act as distributors for some companies. Also, many of the professional teams, the league officers, and the National Collegiate Athletic Association will offer films. Because of variety of sources of media materials, the prospective teachers of minicourses should consult *Free and Inexpensive Materials in Physical Education.*

Bulletin Board Materials

Bulletin boards can be designed to promote the study of sports literature as well as related courses. Similar rules and techniques common to all bulletin boards apply in their construction—creativity, continuity, imagination, and, most importantly, determination and aggressiveness in pursuit of free and inexpensive materials for posting. Obvious sources such as book jackets and action pictures of athletes cut from magazines, newspapers, and sports catalogues constitute a good starting point. Professional teams and college publicity offices generally supply pictures of players free of charge in limited numbers to the public as part of their promotional program. These can frequently be coordinated with books about the sport or athlete and have natural appeal to students. Most companies that sell sports products make available at no cost yearbooks, pamphlets, and booklets to potential customers. Typical materials available are "Quarterback Maneuvers," a photo chart with explanation especially designed for bulletin boards, (Pennsylvania Athletic Equipment—General Tire and Rubber), "Fundamentals for Better Basketball," a short booklet with charts (Converse) and "Exercises and Basketball Tips for Future Stars," a short book of information and illustrations (Bata Bullets). Teachers can work with coaches, athletic directors, and players to obtain these. They are easily obtained by a letter on school stationery or by a 'phone call, and most companies are only too willing to cooperate.[2] Selections from some commercially available bulletin board materials—"Let's Look at Sports Chart Series" (Instructor) and "Physical Activity Charts" (Athletic Institute)—can highlight a display quite nicely.

Exposé and Protest

One of the noticeable trends in athletics in recent years has been the willingness of the players to break with their traditional image and criticize the sports establishment and challenge previous unquestionable procedures. This has taken the form of legal actions, early retirements, protests, strikes, and several articles and books. Dave Meggyesy's *Out of Their League* (Ramparts Press) typically represents the category of expose and protest books. Meggyesy, a successful high school, college, and professional football player, quit the St. Louis Cardinal team following the 1969 season. He had become disillusioned with the brutality, dehumanization, and lack of morality in sports. His book explains his transition from a "gung-ho" athlete to one who questioned the system. A paperback by Paul Hock, *Rip Off the Big Game: The Exploitations of Sports by the Power Elite* (Anchor Books) examines and criticizes in great detail the abuses in sports, such as, financial practices, sexist and racial attitudes, and the brutality imposed upon athletes by some coaches. Harry Edwards, college professor and one of the leading spokespersons for black athletes, has given the case of prevailing racism in sports in his *Revolt of the Black Athlete* (The Free Press). Edwards has presented the reader with a historical development of the black athlete and many specific examples of racism in athletics at all levels. Former New York Yankee baseball pitcher Jim Bouton shocked the sporting world in 1970 with his *Ball Four*, an exposé of the on-and-off field behavior of baseball players, in particular, the New York Yankees. Other players also have written works critical of their sport and some of the excesses connected with it—Curt Flood's *The Way It Is* (Trident Press), Bernie Parrish's *They Call It a Game* (Dial Press), and Johnny Sample's *Confessions of a Dirty Ball Player* (Dial Press) are some examples. Prudence should be the guide in suggesting books to students in this category as some are extremely negative but do contain mature subject matter. Some students can profit from reading them, others cannot.

Summary

The above categories are designed as an example of how a body of knowledge or a subject area can be divided to aid the instructor and the student to design instruction. This can be particularly valuable for the teacher who is inexperienced in the subject area. The interdisciplinary nature of minicourses partially accounts for their popularity and should be listed as one of its advantages.

This sample mini can also serve as the framework for minicourses in sports literature and related areas. Several authors have pointed out the aimlessness of American youth. While this is undoubtedly an overgeneralization, there are many young people who seem to be just marking time. Frequently, teenagers themselves complain, "I have nothing to do. There's nothing to do." Sports literature can open the world of books and provide a wonderful opportunity for these youngsters and even stimulate some to the point of getting them involved in sports. The growth of athletics at every school level offers something of interest for the student. In addition to the traditional major sports, a growing number of which are now available to women, there has been a noticeable increase in womens' sports. Additionally, minor sports (soccer, weight lifting, wrestling) and lifetime sports (golf, Ping-Pong, camping) have greatly developed in recent years. Literally, there is something for everyone. Several books of interest to students that are concerned about women's sports, minor sports, and lifetime sports have already been mentioned in this chapter; others are indicated in the annotated bibliography that follows. The diversity in this field obviously makes it attractive to students. Teachers can also profit from this as the number of educational materials that can be used to achieve their instructional objectives are legion.[3] The bibliography that follows should further illustrate the opportunities the field can provide.

Annotated Bibliography

Fiction

Armer, Alberta. *Screwball*. World, 1963. The story contrasts twin brothers—one an athlete, the other crippled. As the latter attempts to compete with his brother, his mechanical skill brings his success in the Detroit Soap Box Derby.

Bishop, Curtis. *Lonesome End*. Lippincott, 1963. The author explains how Jim, who has experienced many disappointments, finally helps his football team in two important games. Good for young teenagers learning to understand themselves, others, and their world. Some of Bishop's other fine works are *Rebound* and *Sideline Quarterback*.

Brennan, Joe. *Hot Rod Thunder*. Doubleday, 1962. The author emphasizes that hotrodding can be a useful hobby when the rules are followed. A quick moving story that will find a home among many teenagers.

Carson, John. *Hotshot*. Dell, 1961. A well-written, fast-moving book about the adjustment to success of Dave York, a hotshot basketball player. Dave struggles with academics and relationships with women on the way to success.

Christopher, Matt. *Jinx Glove*. Little, Brown, 1974. One of the fine authors of books for young people; this one deals with a young boy's problem with a new baseball glove and how he solves it. The author has written over forty books for young people, which have long been well received by librarians and young people.

Coombs, Charles. *Drag Racing*. Morrow, 1970. Illustrated with 40 photographs and written for the reluctant reader, this book will be a natural for many teenagers.

Deegan, Paul. *The Tournaments*. Creative Education, 1973. Part of the Dan Murphy sport stories series, the author tells the story of how Dan helps his team get into and win the state tournament. The author writes in a simplified form that should appeal to the retarded reader, yet shows a good knowledge of the techniques of the game. This series should appeal to the intermediate level student and up.

Felsen, H. G. *Hot Rod*. Bantam, 1950. A natural for teenagers, the author has composed a work with a fast-moving and interesting plot with emphasis on safety.

Fleming, Alice. *Hosannah, the Home Run*. Little, Brown, 1972. This author has written thirty-four poems on many aspects of sports; illustrations enhance the book.

Frick, Constance H. *Patch*. Harcourt, 1957. The story of a record-breaking track star. The author combines humor and serious writing in telling the maturation of the main character.

Gilbert, Nan. *Champions Don't Cry*. Harper, Row and Company, 1960. Sally, a teenage tennis player, learns that self-control is essential if she wishes to be a champion.

Henry, Marguerite. *King of the Wind*. Rand McNally, 1948. The story of a horse and a young boy and the problems they experience together. The book, using North Africa for the setting, is just one of Ms. Henry's books on horses. This one was awarded the Newberry Medal.

Honig, Donald. *Johnny Lee.* McCall, 1971. The story of the experiences of a Black player in his rookie season. During his first year in baseball as a minor league player in Virginia he is confronted with discrimination but also makes wonderful friendships.

Kessler, Leonard. *Here Comes the Strikeout.* Harper and Row, 1965. Both relations between the races and perserverance to achieve success form the background of this story. Willie, a Black player, is correcting his faults as a batter and getting a hit. This book for the beginning reader is part of the "Sports I Can Read" series by the same author; others include *Kick, Pass and Run* and *The Last One Is a Rotten Egg.*

Knott, Bill. *Junk Pitcher.* Follett, 1963. The account of a young pitcher who makes it to the major leagues only to be sent down to the minors for further development. The author emphasizes that not only is talent important to success but desire and drive as well. An exciting, valuable, and accurate work.

Konigsburg, E. L. *About the B'Nai Bagels.* Atheneum, 1975. A humorous interesting well-done story that deals with human relations and moral dilemmas. The smooth but fast-flowing plot will hold the reader's attention.

Lipsyte, Robert. *The Contender.* Bantam, 1967. Lipsyte has written a fast-moving story of a Harlem youth, who spends his time avoiding both street conflicts and fists in the boxing ring.

Lord, Beman. *Shrimp's Soccer Goal.* Walck, 1969. A soccer story, unusual in not only treating a minor sport, but in the fact that the founder and coach of the team is a woman.

Neigoff, Mike. *Nine Make a Team.* Whitman, 1963. The importance of cooperation and team play serves as the focus for this book. In it, a young boy learns its importance for success.

Ogan, Margaret and George. *Donavan's Dusters.* Westminster Press, 1975. One of the few stories on motorcycle racing containing good action and excitement.

Olgin, Joseph. *Backcourt Atom.* Houghton, 1960. Initially it would seem that Shorty McLean's problem is his size in terms of his future as a basketball player. However, cooperation and learning to make friends are the real stumbling blocks he had to overcome to be a champion.

Phillips, Maurice. *Lightning on Ice.* Doubleday, 1963. A hockey story in which the main character, Kim Morgan, learns the relationship of sports to sportsmanship.

Sankey, Alice. *Basketballs for Breakfast.* Whitman, 1963. Following the loss of his position on the junior high basketball team, Larry fears he may never play again. He joins a group at the YMCA and proceeds to learn more about the sport and again plays for the team.

Savitz, Harriet May. *Fly, Wheels, Fly!* The John Day Company, 1970. Dedicated to the Norristown Central Penn Wheelers, the author weaves a story of two young boys, both paralyzed, who join a group of sports paraplegics for the Paralympics. Experiencing both success and failure, the boys realize their lives need not be confined though they are physically confined to their chairs.

Shortall, Leonard. *Ben on the Ski Trail.* Morrow, 1965. One of the few fictional stories on skiing which follows a boy's first attempts at learning to ski.

Summer, Richard. *The Ballshy Pitcher.* Steck-Vaughn Co., 1970. Summer's story is characterized by two themes—ballshyness, which is fear of being hit and hurt by the ball, and ethnic and racial harmony as whites, Blacks and Mexicans learn the value of working together.

Walden, Amelia. *Go, Phillips, Go!* Westminster Press, 1974. The story of Pete, a teenage girl who plays for the basketball team. The plot covers all the typical problems of adolescence as well as that of a women athlete.

Technical

Anderson, Clary. *Make the Team in Baseball.* Grosset and Dunlap, 1960. Well-written, how-to book containing sketches and pictures of the various aspects of the game. The author has dissected the game and provided in a readable style suggestions for the athlete, from batting grip to "competitive spirit."

Angier, Bradford, and Taylor, Zack. *Introduction to Canoeing.* Stackpole, 1973. For the canoeing enthusiast, this nicely done manual contains a significant amount of information for the novice or the expert.

Auerbach, Arnold. *Basketball for the Player, the Fan and the Coach.* Simon and Schuster, 1975. "Red" has rewritten a book that originally appeared in 1972 that contains information about a sport that he has helped to develop. The technical information is handled in a popular style making it useful for all those who enjoy basketball.

Bee, Clair. *Basketball for Everyone.* Ace Books, 1962. One of the few books prepared for the player, fan, and coach by one of the few persons able to do it—Clair Bee, successful coach and prolific author. The book contains everything from "how to watch a game" to scouting.

———. *Make the Team in Basketball.* Grosset and Dunlap, 1961. A classic how-to book that explains basketball in understandable terms for the beginning player. The author, a successful coach and writer, has included many pictures and sketches to simplify the book.

Bethel, Dell. *Inside Baseball.* Reilly and Lee Brooks, 1968. The author has put together a book that attempts to provide information for each position on a baseball team. Particularly well done is the chapter on "situations" that explains the duty of each player for various game situations. Best used at the high school level.

Bridge, Raymond. *Free Wheeling: The Bicycle Camping Book.* Stackpole, 1974. With the explosion of bike tours this book will be very popular. Not only well written but also contains pictures and diagrams explaining technical points. Well done and comprehensive.

Canham, Don. *Cross Country Techniques Illustrated.* Ronald Press, 1953. A basic approach that explains the form and training techniques used in track. It contains excellent detail for the person wishing to run track, but there is only minimal information on diet, rest and training aids.

Clause, Frank and Patty McBride. *The Complete Handbook of Junior Bowling.* Fleet Publishing, 1964. An extremely useful, interesting, and valuable book for the bowling novice. A large part of the book details equipment, keeping score and similar basics.

Cuthbertson, Tom. *Bike Tripping.* Ten Speed Press, 1972. A light yet thorough treatment of biking. The author gives many pages of tips and sound advice so as to avoid problems and have success.

Frey, Shaney. *The Complete Beginner's Guide to Skin Diving.* Doubleday, 1965. An easy to read, well-illustrated book on the fundamentals of a sport that has become very popular in recent years. The book also contains additional information of the sea creatures.

Gottlieb, William. *Table Tennis.* Knopf, 1954. A fundamental and basic approach to the game covering such aspects as equipment, rules, tactics and spin strokes. Generally it is a very useful book for the beginner with descriptive pictures and illustrations.

Granda, Julio. *The First Book of Basketball.* Franklin Watts, 1959. Especially appealing to the novice player or useful in encouraging a prospective player, this book introduces the game to the reader. Explaining the equipment, rules, and techniques in a nonthreatening, readable style, accompanied by illustrations, the author educates as well as excites the reader about the sport. Others in this series are equally as good: for example, *The First Book of Football* and *The First Book of Baseball* for the young reader.

Jacobs, G., and McCrory, J. R. *Baseball Rules in Pictures.* Grosset and Dunlap, 1973. A simplified, well-illustrated, step-by-step explanation of the rules of the game. Each rule contains several sketches, thus showing it visually. There are several other fine books in this series such as *Softball Rules in Pictures.* These are helpful not only to players, managers, and officials but also to fans.

Leighton, Jim. *Inside Tennis: Techniques of Winning.* Prentice-Hall, 1969. Providing information for the beginner, intermediate, and advanced player, the author, a teaching professional, aided by several other contributors details fundamentals to strategy. A good choice for purchase because of its applicability to all ability levels.

Liss, Howard. *Basketball Talk for Beginners.* Messner, 1970. Liss, an experienced sports author, provides a dictionary approach to the terminology of the game. Illustrations explain the more difficult concepts. A good library addition for the young reader.

McNally, Tom. *Fishing for Boys.* Follett, 1962. Over forty million people in this country enjoy fishing—the author provides a book of how to do it advice for the beginner. In addition to fundamentals, he also includes information on ice fishing, types of fish, and knots useful to the person wishing to fish.

Mann, Arthur. *How to Play Winning Baseball.* Grosset and Dunlap, 1953. Illustrated with over 100 sketches, this book covers all topics related to the game. Of particular value are the chapters on pitching, which is examined in great detail.

Masin, Herman. *How to Star in Football.* Scholastic, 1966. A basic well-illustrated short book containing many helpful hints, exercises, and ideas on how to be a successful football player.

Messner, Reinhold. *The Seventh Grade.* Oxford University Press, 1973. The book contains the autobiographic experiences of the author, a mountain climber. He explains some of his climbs; several striking pictures of his various climbs illustrate the book.

Owen, Maribel Vinson. *The Fun of Figure Skating.* Harper and Row, 1960. A primer on figure skating, the book provides specific suggestions on the techniques needed as well as the steps, spins, and dances if one is to become a polished figure skater.

Paterson, Ann, editor. *Team Sports for Girls.* Ronald Press, 1958. Beginning with a justification of the value of team sports by the editor, several authors in turn explain the rules, facilities, and equipment necessary and fundamentals for several women's team sports. This book is useful for its excellent attention to detail and skill development.

Percival, Lloyd. *The Hockey Handbook.* A. S. Barnes, 1961. A sophisticated how-to book for intermediate hockey players—not for beginners. The book is notable for its lack of pictures and great attention to specifics.

Quington, Ray. *Basic Fly Fishing and Fly Tying.* Stackpole, 1973. A comprehensive paperback that contains an enormous amount of information and diagrams for fly fishing.

Ramsey, Jack. *Pressure Basketball.* Prentice-Hall, 1963. One of the truly fine technical books on the defensive aspects of basketball by a coach of college and professional basketball teams. Diagrams and step-by-step pictures simplify the complex aspects of the book.

Ryan, Frank. *Weight Training.* Viking, 1969. A well-illustrated book that points out the value of weight training to muscle development. The book details the traditional approach and avoids some of the more modern approaches.

Schiffer, Don. *First Book of Football.* Franklin Watts, 1958. Although dated, the basic material in the book remains useful to the young reader; diagrams explain various aspects of the game, plays, and officials' hand signals. Other books in the series are equally as useful—*Baseball* (Brewster, 1970), *Basketball* (Schiffer, 1959), *Ice Hockey* (Whitehead, 1964).

Silks, Donald. *Boxing for Boys.* Knopf, 1953. The author provides information on the sport including basic fundamentals, training practices, and training techniques.

Sports Illustrated. *Basketball.* Lippincott, 1971. Clearly the outstanding book for the high school player and spectator, it contains explanations with accompanying diagrams, charts, and pictures. Extremely well-written, it covers some complex topics nicely. This is part of a series, *Football Offense, Horseback Riding, Training with Weights, Squash,* and others by *Sports Illustrated,* the sports magazine.

Sports Techniques Book Series. Athletic Institute. A series of books on many sports, major and minor, that are particularly helpful to the student with reading difficulties. Each book contains drawings, pictures, and illustrations for clarification. *Golf, Women's Track and Field, Bowling,* and *Ice Hockey* are some of the titles.

Tyll, Al. *The Complete Beginner's Guide to Water Skiing.* Doubleday, 1970. The author provides the reader with a comprehensive manual for the sport with chapters from preservation of skis and kite flying to history and water rules. Several pictures illustrate the work.

General Interest

Arlott, John. *Oxford Companion to World Sports and Games.* Oxford, 1975. An excellent ready reference, done in dictionary format, with the purpose of providing a brief understanding of a sport, its history, nature, techniques, and personalities. It excludes "blood" sports as well as detailed rules of the games covered.

Arthur, Lee; James, Elizabeth and Taylor, Judith. *Sportsmath: How It Works.* Lothrop, Lee and Shepard, 1975. The authors use several sports as examples and discuss how statistics for players are compiled—for example, batting average, yards per pass completed and field goal percentage.

Associated Press Sports Staff. *A Century of Sports.* Plimpton Press, 1971. Examines the major developments and personalities in the world of sports over the last 100 years. Covers many minor sports—judo, rowing, polo, field hockey, and rodeo.

Barr, George. *Here's Why: Science in Sports.* Scholastic, 1962. Well-written and illustrated text explaining how sports uses science to meet its requirements, using examples such as curve balls, spiral passes, and high jumping.

Beers, Paul B. *Profiles in Pennsylvania Sports.* Stackpole Books, 1975. A well-done history of sport figures in the state that covers some historical figures but mainly contemporary personalities of all races and both sexes. Many other states have similar books dealing with sports figures that are native sons.

Bennett, Margaret. *Cross-Country Skiing for the Fun of It.* Ballantine, 1973. Using a step-by-step approach beginning with equipment, the author provides a wealth of information on everything from parks and weather to clubs.

Bewagh, Jim. *Incredible Athletic Feats.* Hart, 1969. Examples: Dean landed a 2,664 lb. shark with hook and rod, Ernst walked from Constantinople to Calcutta and back in 59 days, Brown beat 6 fighters on the same night, Mildred Diedrickson Zaharias was a champion in track, golf, and baseball.

Biever, Vernon, and Biever, John E. *Meet the Coaches.* Creative Educational Society, 1975. Visually oriented and aimed at the primary school student, it explains the careers of four successful coaches. The book is inspirational as it explains the adversity each overcame on his way to success. Other books in the series are *Meet the Quarterbacks, Meet the Running Backs, Meet the Linebackers, Meet the Receivers, and Meet the Defensive Lineman.* An advanced form of each book, for the intermediate grade student, is produced by the same publisher under the series title "Stars of the NFL."

Brash, R. *How Did Sports Begin?* David McKay, 1970. The author treats 45 sports devoting considerable detail to each in a massive volume. Because of the attention to detail and the coverage devoted to many of the very minor sports—croquet, badminton, water polo, it is an excellent book. The author, who has published many other works, did the requisite extensive research necessary to make this an extraordinary book.

Brown, Warren. *Win, Lose or Draw.* Putnam, 1947. The author, an experienced sports writer, tells the story behind the story in this easy flowing book. The book deals with all sports; its value lies in its inside look at sports in the early part of this century.

Burchard, Marshall and Sue. *O. J. Simpson.* Putnam, 1975. One of the "Sports Hero" series by the same author and publisher. The book, written for the primary school student, is set in large type and contains several illustrations. Others in the series, *Richard Petty, Reggie Jackson, Johnny Bench,* and others are equally as well done.

Butler, Hal. *There's Nothing New in Sports.* Messner, 1967. A compact history of both major and minor sports popular in the U.S. The author, who has written several short stories, has written in a somewhat advanced style and, thus, the book would be most useful to upper level high school students.

_____. *Underdogs of Sport.* Messner, 1969. Examples: "1913—Miracle at West Point (Notre Dame vs. Army) Forward Pass"; "1963—Night the Peasants Beat the Kings (Loyola vs. Cincinnati)." Includes football, baseball, boxing, basketball, golf, hockey, and horse racing.

The Complete Book of Pro Basketball. Lancer. A yearly publication that covers the statistics, rookies, and outlook for each team. The annual usually contains two or three articles from coaches or players about various aspects of the game. A good choice for an inexpensive (paperback) reference work.

Connelly, Thomas L. *Discovering the Appalachians.* Stackpole, 1968. An intensive description of the Appalachians that will be of interest to the beginning or advanced bicycle rider or backpacker. The book contains several pictures and maps.

Cummings, Parke. *The Dictionary of Sports.* Ronald Press, 1949. Organized in dictionary form, the book defines terms from all sports; includes regular and slang terms.

Davis, Mac. *Strange and Incredible Sports Happenings.* Grosset and Dunlap, 1975. A fascinating collection of truly unusual events that have occurred in sports—"The Jockey Who Came Back From the Dead," "Baseball's Strangest Mystery"; written in a light, readable fashion sure to interest both the fan and nonfan.

Davis, Mary. *Careers in Baseball.* Learner, 1973. Written for the primary school student, these career education books focus on the usher, manager, player, and others and their relation to the game. With each job description there is a picture. Also in this series are the following sports books: *Careers in Football* and *Careers in Hockey.*

Durant, John. *The Sports of Our Presidents.* Macmillan, 1962. Beginning with George Washington's fox hunting, the author describes the sports of the presidents. The book details the interests of each of the men who have occupied the White House, from George Washington's fox hunting to President Kennedy's touch football and President Johnson's deer hunting.

_____. *Highlights of the World Series.* Hastings House, 1973. One of several books by the author in which he examines the historical development of a sport—changes, trends, pictures, and commentary. Durant's books (several published by Hastings House) make good reference selections.

_____, and Bettman, Otto. *Pictorial History of American Sports.* A. S. Barnes, 1965. Heavily detailed with pictures and illustrations, the text presents both an informative and interesting history of the development of sports. The general emphasis has been placed on the recent years and the major sports.

Goldstein, Norm. *Touchdowns and $$$$: The New Athlete.* Scott Generation, 1973. This special report (a cassette filmstrip) examines the changes in modern sports and modern athletes. The business aspects of sports are emphasized. Particularly good for high school students.

Hall, Al, editor. *Complete Guide to the Bicycle*. Peterson, 1975. A series of articles ranging from a history of the development of the bicycle to a guide for buyers. Of particular interest are the chapters on a 140-mile-an-hour bike record and the physical benefits of the sport; many pictures and diagrams are included.

Harkins, Philip. *Where the Shark Waits*. Morrow, 1963. Although written a dozen years before the "Jaws" mania, this story will be of particular interest. Most of the action takes place underwater in California and Mexico as the hero, a young skin diver, faces sharks.

Harris, H. A. *Greek Athletes and Athletics*. Indiana University Press, 1964. The author explains the role and development of athletics in Greece as well as the events in which women and men participated. May be useful as a springboard to interest the athlete or sports fan in the early history of athletics.

————. *Sport in Greece and Rome*. Cornell University, 1972. The author explains the nature and organization of sports during the classical era. Because of the amount of detail and scholarly approach, it may be useful to the sports enthusiast who also enjoys reading history.

Hillary, Sir Edmund. *Nothing Venture, Nothing Win*. Coward, McCann and Geoghegan, 1975. The author, an adventurer, and explorer (he was the first man to conquer Mount Everest), writes an autobiographical account with an emphasis on his mountain climbing activities.

Holliman, Jennie. *American Sports*. Porcupine Press, 1975. The author has put together a short book that explains the nature of the sports engaged in by Americans in the first years of the country's existence. While interesting in itself, it may be useful to interest the reader in early American history.

Hot Rod Yearbook, Number 12. Peterson, 1972. One of the most popular books among teenagers in the library, this annual book covers many of the topics of interest to those interested in customizing their cars. The following are sample chapters: "Racing Roundup," "100 Ways to Beat Inflation," and "Stuckup Customizing."

Kamm, Herbert. *The New Junior Illustrated Encyclopedia Sports*. Bobbs-Merrill, 1975. A useful source for the younger student, this work contains an abundance of information on the history, players, and records of professional and college sports.

Keith, Harold. *Sports and Games*. Corwell, 1969. Most recent revision of a handbook on major and minor sports covering rules, achievements as well as some useful information on techniques for improvement of the athlete or casual player.

Koppett, Leonard. *New York Times Guide to Spectator Sports*. Quadrangle Books, 1971. The author answers many of the questions that spectators have when watching sports. Easy reading with information on most sports (football, basketball, horse racing, golf, tennis, gymnastics, wrestling) and excellent illustrations characterize the books.

Kuenster, John, editor. *From Cobb to "Catfish."* Rand McNally, 1975. A collection of 128 articles that appeared in Baseball Digest that are guaranteed to hold the interest of player, fan, or even the casually sports-minded.

Lincoln Library of Sports Champions. Frontier Press, 1974. A multivolume work that continues to be one of the most popular items in every library.

McWhirter, Norris and Ross. *Guinness Sports Record Books*. Sterling, 1975. The Guinness books continue to be some of the most popular in the library and this is no exception.

Menke, Frank. *The Encyclopedia of Sports*. A. S. Barnes, 1963. An encyclopedia approach to all sports with descriptions of each. A useful reference tool for rules, statistical data and the development of the sport for both major and minor sports.

Morton, Henry W. *Soviet Sport*. Crowell-Collier, 1963. Sport in Soviet society must serve a purposeful function in order to justify its continued existence. This book explains Soviet sports and should be popular in view of the continuing visits by Soviet teams and the Olympics.

Peterson, Robert. *Only the Ball Was White*. Prentice-Hall, 1970. Until relatively recently (the last 25 years) Black athletes were excluded from professional baseball. With excerpts from several players who played in the Negro leagues or with barnstorming Negro teams, the author paints an interesting picture of life before Jackie Robinson.

Riggs, Bobby. *Court Hustler*. Lippincott, 1973. The author has written his memories of how he has hustled money through betting and why he has done so. The book, which is entertaining and humorous, contains some pointers on how to play tennis.

Rooney, John R. *A Geography of American Sport: From Cabin Creek to Anaheim*. Addison-Wesley, 1974. The author has analyzed the various areas of the country and mapped the sports interests of each region. It may be somewhat of a help in settling sports discussions as well as interesting to the athlete.

Rosenberg, John M. *The Story of Baseball*. Random House, 1966. Beginning with the early days of the sport, the author explains the development of the sport in a well-written, readable style. Major figures and teams are highlighted; many outstanding and classic pictures are contained in the book.

Schaap, Richard. *An Illustrated History of the Olympics*. Knopf, 1963. A beautifully illustrated, well-written history of the Olympic games and the athletes. The back of the book contains tables on Olympic statistics.

Shapiro, Milton J. *A Treasury of Sports Humor*. Messner, 1972. A collection of interesting and humorous anecdotes by a well-published sports author. The stories cover the main sports, mainly baseball, but also horse racing, basketball, golf, hockey, and football.

Smith, Chet, and Wolfson, Marty. *Pittsburgh and Western Pennsylvania Sports Hall of Fame*. Wolfson, 1969. Covering contemporary as well as historical teams, players, and topics, this book has particular regional appeal. Some comparable books are available for other regions of the country that will also be of considerable interest to readers of all ages.

Turkin, Hy, and Thompson, S. C. *The Official Encyclopedia of Baseball*. A. S. Barnes, 1963. An extremely well-researched and heavily detailed work that exists as an excellent reference for the sport. It includes statistics on every player that has played the game as well as the more common items—home run records, Hall of Fame, etc.

Walker, Henry. *Illustrated Baseball Dictionary for Young People*. Harvey House, 1970. Clearly one of the finest books available for young people. Arranged in dictionary style, the book explains popular terms in a simple, easily understood fashion. The illustrations clarify the explanation. A recent companion volume, *Illustrated Football Dictionary for Young People* by Joseph Olgin is equally as well done.

Biography and Autobiography

Berger, Phil. *Joe Namath: Maverick Quarterback*. Regnery, 1969. One of the most popular and well-known quarterbacks in contemporary football is Namath, quarterback for the New York Jets football team. This book highlights the exploits of this popular player.

Devaney, John. *Tom Seaver*. Popular Library, 1974. An in-depth study of one of baseball's most successful and exciting pitchers. Several anecdotes provide good insight to his off-the-field activities.

Farr, Finis. *Black Champion*. Fawcett, 1969. Jack Johnson was the first Black boxing champion; the author tells his story and relates the problems as well as the successes.

Gibson, Althea, and Fitzgerald, Edward. *I Always Wanted to Be Somebody*. Harper and Row, 1968. Born and raised in New York's Harlem, this Black woman tells the story of her life and her rise to status as the finest women's tennis player in the country and one of the best in the world. A warm, well-written book that also discusses the integration of what is still today a white sport.

Gibson, Bod, and Pepe, Phil. *From Ghetto to Glory: The Story of Bob Gibson*. Prentice-Hall, 1968. The story of the rise of Bob Gibson to become a fine pitcher on the St. Louis Cardinals baseball team, from his boyhood. Inspirational and human story of interest to young people of all types of backgrounds.

Gutstskey, Earl. *Roman Gabriel, Outstanding Pro*. Grosset and Dunlap, 1974. This book can be particularly helpful to the aspiring athlete because of its emphasis in the importance of conditioning to success. This series, "Sports Shelf Books"—*Tom Seaver of the Mets, Manny Sanguillen: Jolly Pirate, Kareem: Basketball Great*, and others are particularly well-written and appealing to the high school student and those older.

Jackson, Robert J. *Earl the Pearl: The Story of Baltimore's Earl Monroe*. Walck, 1969. Earl Monroe, presently playing on the New York Knicks basketball team, has particularly strong following among inner city Black youths. This book tells his story from the playgrounds of Philadelphia to his success with the Baltimore Bullets. Jackson has written several biographies, such as *Supermex* and *Let's Go, Yaz*, for young people.

Jacobs, Linda. *Annemarie Proell*. EMC, 1975. A short biographical account with pictures of a successful skier that will be interesting to the young reader.

Kramer, Jerry. *Farewell to Football*. World, 1969. A member of the perennial football champions Green Bay Packers and himself a former perennial All-Pro player, he focuses on the field and the concurrent pains as he explains the factors in his decision to retire. He has also written *Instant Replay*.

Libby, Bill, and Haywood, Spencer. *Stand Up for Something: The Spencer Haywood Story*. Grosset and Dunlap, 1972. One of the eleven children born in Silver City, Mississippi, Haywood used basketball as a vehicle for upward social and financial mobility. At age 23, he was earning over $200,000 a year. The authors chronicled his life in the rural South through the ghettos of Chicago and Detroit to success in college, the Olympics, and the pro's.

Lieb, Frederick. *Connie Mack: Grand Old Man of Baseball.* G. P. Putnam's Sons, 1945. The life story of baseball's great Connie Mack, player, manager, and owner. The author provides insights to the game as it developed while explaining the contribution of Mack. Several classic pictures are included.

Mantle, Mickey. *The Education of a Baseball Player.* Simon and Schuster, 1967. The story of the initiation and assimilation of one of baseball's great stars in the game. He tells of his fears (and later successes) when as a rural boy he began his career. It should be interesting to baseball fans and to rural students.

Owens, Jesse, with Paul Neimark. *Blackthink.* Morrow, 1970. An autobiographical account of his athletic feats and off-the-field activities. He also speaks on racism, black-white relations, and black militance.

Piersall, Jim, and Hirshberg, Al. *Fear Strikes Out.* Little, Brown, 1955. One of the greatest comeback stories in sports history. It relates in the author's own words his recovery from mental illness.

Ruth, Babe, and Considine, Bob. *The Babe Ruth Story.* Scholastic, 1948. The dramatic rags-to-riches story of one of baseball's great legends and holder of many baseball records.

Ryback, Eric. *The High Adventure of Eric Ryback.* Bantam, 1971. The account of the 2,300 mile journey of the 18-year-old author. Traveling by foot from Canada to Mexico, he recounts his high adventure.

Sayers, Gale, and Silverman, Al. *I Am Third.* Bantam, 1970. Authored by a former football great who reviews his career—its pains, problems and success, his friendship with Brian Piccolo, and his religious faith.

Schollander, Don, and Savage, Michael. *Deep Water.* Crown Publishers, 1971. The author, an Olympic swimming champion, tells of the demands made upon successful athletes. Schollander, who writes the book with his Yale roommate, describes in minute detail some of the daily events in the life of a successful athlete and what is required in terms of public appearances and training.

Thorne, Alice. *Clemente.* Grosset and Dunlap, 1973. The biography of a Puerto Rican baseball player, Roberto Clemente, fills the pages of this short book designed for young readers. Parts of the Thistle series, others include *Jim Plunkett, Csonka, Billie Jean King,* that can be especially appealing to the reluctant reader.

Wilson, Beth. *Muhammed Ali.* Putnam, 1974. A "See and Read Biography" of the championship boxer, both in the Olympics and professionals. This book will be of particular value to the novice reader because of the simplified style and the many drawings accompanying the narrative.

Wolfe, Dave. *Foul! Connie Hawkins, Schoolyard Star, Exile NBA Superstar.* Holt, Rinehart and Winston, 1972. His college career tainted by possible relationships with gamblers, "the Hawk" was barred from the NBA, the established professional league. Hawkins graduated from Boys High in Brooklyn and the school yards of New York City to eventually play in the NBA, but, only after pressure had been applied legally and publically to admit him.

Young, Bernice. *The Picture Story of Frank Robinson.* Messner, 1975. Part of a series, this book about baseball's first Black team manager details the career and early life of Frank Robinson. Because of the topic, the pictures, and the easy reading, it and others in the series should find a home with the young reader or the student with reading problems.

Anthologies

Bontemps, Arna. *Famous Negro Athletes.* Dodd, Mead, 1969. This anthology is of particular interest and value because of its treatment of successful Black athletes in major as well as minor sports.

Boy's Life Book of Sports Stories. Random House, 1965. The editors have compiled the stories from *Boy's Life* magazines. Illustrated by Don Miller, the stories make easy, fast-paced reading. The stories are traditional but particularly appealing to young boys.

Davis, Mac. *Baseball's Unforgettables.* Bantam, 1966. Davis has compiled an excellent collection of short little stories and anecdotes most of which are nothing short of amazing.

Gelman, Steve. *Young Olympic Champions.* W. W. Norton, 1964. A truly interesting description of the successes of eleven young athletes in the Olympics. The author covers American men (Johnny Weissmuller, Jerry Lucas) and women (Wilma Rudolph, Sonja Henie) as well as a few foreign champions.

Hollander, Phyllis. *American Women in Sports.* Grosset and Dunlap, 1972. This anthology, divided on the basis of each sport, covers the activities of many women athletes. Bowling, Olympic skiing, and horseback riding are some of the sports the author examines in terms of female participation.

———, and Hollander, Zander. *They Dared to Lead: America's Black Athletes.* Grosset and Dunlap, 1972. An excellent series of short original articles by fine authors. The articles focus on the personal lives as well as professional successes and their contribution of their chosen sport.

Hyde, Margaret and Edwin. *Where Speed Is King.* McGraw-Hill, 1961. The authors devote each of the 10 chapters to an aspect of speed. Beginning with the "fastest men in the world," they cover such topics as horses, boats, pigeons, hot rods, soap boxes, and spaceships in relation to speed.

Lorimer, Lawrence, editor. *Breaking In.* Random House, 1974. The author has put together from books nine first-person accounts of athletes and their descriptions of how they learned to cope with excitement, apprehension, pain, and success of sports. Autobiographical accounts are from Spencer Haywood, Althea Gibson, and Jackie Robinson, as well as six others.

McKay, Don, editor. *Wild Wheels.* Dell, 1968. An anthology devoted to racing and edited by a reading specialist. The well-selected readings should be found particularly interesting by teenagers who are especially interested in "hot cars."

Mantle, Mickey. *The Quality of Courage.* Banner, 1964. This collection of true stories of courage, bravery, and heroism using examples from baseball will be inspirational to the young athlete who has suffered reverses.

Marsh, Irving T., and Ehre, Edward. *Best Sports Stories.* E. P. Dutton, 1975. The editors, aided by sports writers serving as judges, have pulled together an outstanding collection of essays from magazines and newspapers and several excellent photographs. The series, which has now appeared since 1944, covers both the major and minor sports as well as several general sports articles.

Owen, Frank, editor. *Teenage Sport Stories*. Latern. A nice collection of stories that will provide interesting reading to young people.

Talamini, John T., and Page, Charles H. *Sports and Society*. Little, Brown, 1973. An outstanding collection of readings on the role of sports in American society. The anthology includes some original pieces as well as excerpts from books and reprints of articles from a diverse selection of authors such as Harry Edwards, Jerry Kramer, President John Kennedy, and Roger Bannister. Examples are "The Black Athlete on the College Campus," "The Affluent Baseball Player," "The Soft American" and "Women Athletes."

Newspapers

Basketball News. 114 Madison Avenue, Coral Gables, Florida 33134. A weekly newspaper that contains statistical and extensive information on all aspects of the sport. It appeals more to the player than to the spectator.

Basketball Weekly. 19830 Mack Avenue, Grosse Pointe, Michigan 48236. A weekly newspaper published seasonally that contains an enormous amount of information on basketball. In addition to statistical information, each issue contains in-depth articles on teams, coaches, and players at the secondary, college, and professional level.

Football News. 19830 Mack Avenue, Grosse Pointe, Michigan 48236. Published weekly during the season, this newspaper covers every aspect of the sport from high school to college. Each issue contains in-depth articles on coaches, players, and teams.

Sporting News. 1212 North Lindbergh, St. Louis, Missouri 63166. A weekly newspaper that focuses on each sport as it is in season. Emphasis of coverage is on major sports at the professional and collegiate level. Excellent source of statistical information (e.g., baseball batting averages).

Magazines

Athletic Journal. 1719 Howard Street, Evanston, Illinois 60202. Containing many articles written by successful coaches, this technical journal is read by many coaches, athletes and sports fans.

The Basketball Clinic. Parker Publishing Company, West Nyack, New York 10994. A highly technical and expensive periodical that contains articles by successful coaches. This should be ordered for purchase by libraries where the community is totally committed to basketball. This company published similar journals for the other sports.

Bicycling. 119 Paul Drive, San Rafael, California 94903. With the expansion of the interest in bicycling many librarians will wish to consider this purchase. It contains articles on everything from saddle soreness to desert biking.

Black Sports. 31 East 28th Street, New York, N.Y. 10016. A sports journal that concentrates on Black athletes, mainly professional but also college and high school players. In addition, it contains technical articles, book reviews, and many fine pictures.

Boating. P.O. Box 2773, Boulder, Colorado 80302. A lavishly illustrated and surprisingly well-written and edited magazine that deals with all aspects of maritime life. In addition to containing how-to articles, it also carries adventure, historical, and new items.

Coach and Athlete. 200 S. Hull Street, Montgomery, Alabama 36104. A good sports journal that contains general and technical articles as well as commentary on various developments in sports.

Hot Rod Magazine. Petersen Publishing Co., 5959 Hollywood Blvd., Los Angeles, California 90028. Characterized by pictures of customized cars (regular cars that have been remodeled to look more beautiful or adjusted to go faster), this magazine will have great appeal to the student.

Karate Illustrated. 1847 W. Empire Avenue, Burbank, California 91504. The exposition of interest in the martial arts make this new magazine a consideration. Although some articles place too much emphasis on violence, the magazine generally emphasizes the sports aspect.

Motor Trend Magazine. Petersen Publishing Co., 5959 Hollywood Blvd., Los Angeles, California 90028. This magazine, which emphasizes safety in the design and manufacturing of automobiles, is characterized by pictures and analysis of motor vehicles (gas mileage, handling, braking). Because of the interest in cars by teenagers, this is a good choice for libraries.

Scholastic Coach. Scholastic Coach, Inc., 50 W. 44th St., New York, New York 10036. A fine journal, written predominantly for the coach and the mature player but also should find a home with several spectators. Contains several technical articles.

Skin Diver. Petersen Publishing Co., 5959 Hollywood Blvd., Los Angeles, California 90028. This magazine contains articles on underwater skin diving, on places of interest, equipment and technique.

Sport. MacFaddon-Bartell Corporation, 205 E. 42nd Street, New York, New York 10017. Presently edited by the fine sports journalist, Dick Shapp, this magazine contains many good articles for spectators on the major and minor sports. Articles deal with players, coaches and teams.

Sports Illustrated. 541 North Fairbanks Court, Chicago, Illinois 60611. The largest selling sports magazine that is characterized by fine writing, excellent pictures, and advertisements. While largely devoted to the spectator sports, it covers the minor sports and lesser known schools.

Sports Philadelphia. 1420 Walnut Street, Philadelphia, Pennsylvania 19102. A regional sports magazine that carries articles on teams, players, and coaches in the Delaware Valley area. With the current sports mania, there should be many journals like this springing up around the nation.

Sports Woman. 119 Paul Drive, San Rafael, California 94903. Containing articles on players, coaches, and techniques this magazine seems especially appropriate for today's female athlete.

Swimming World. Swimming World, Inc. 8522 Bellanca, Los Angeles, California 90045. Magazines like this one and others similar to it (*Boating, Ski, World Tennis, Bicycling, Backpacking Journal, Hockey World, Karate Illustrated,* and *Fishing World*) are useful to purchase for libraries where the school or the community has a particular interest in that sport. These magazines contain good pictures, articles, and illustrations on players, coaches, teams, and events.

Track and Field News. P.O. Box 296, Los Altos, California 94022. A journal containing information of interest to athlete and coach. The journal has both technical articles and general information on meets and athletes.

Women Sports. Women's Sport Publishing Company, 1660 S. Amphlet Blvd., San Mateo, California. 50306. With the rise of women's participation in athletics and emergence of women on male teams, this is a very likely library acquisition. It covers players, coaches, teams, and events.

World Tennis. 383 Madison Avenue, New York, New York 10017. For librarians where there is a tennis emphasis in the school or community, this magazine is a must. It contains articles (pictures and diagrams) on the leading figures in the sport and technical essays on how to improve one's game.

Nonprint Media

BFA Educational Media Super 8MM Silent Film Loops. BFA Educational Media, 2211 Michigan Avenue, Santa Monica, California 90404. A series of film loops for several sports (volleyball, handball) with several film loops for each sport. The value of this series lies in the attention to minor sports and detail, and the several films devoted to lifetime sports.

Elementary Physical Education Film Loops. Ealing Films, 2225 Massachusetts Avenue, Cambridge. Massachusetts 02140. This film loop series contains some films that will be useful for self-instruction in the library (throwing and catching arms and abdominal strength). These, in turn, can motivate additional reading.

First Aid. Ealing Films. A series of six sound filmstrips that explain procedures to follow in cases of injury or accident. Should appeal to scouts, athletes, and others interested in first aid.

How to Play Softball. Athletic Institute, 705 Merchandise Mart, Chicago, Illinois 60654. A sound filmstrip with tape cassette that explains with graphics the basic fundamentals and techniques of the sport. This is just one of a new series (1976) produced by the Athletic Institute for the elementary school student that can easily be used by them individually in the library.

Introducing Badminton. National Film Board of Canada. The fundamentals and rules are explained in this color filmstrip with accompanying diagrams and pictures for further clarification.

Introducing Volleyball. National Film Board of Canada. A color filmstrip that contains the rules and fundamentals of the game of volleyball as well as diagrams and pictures to illustrate major points made.

Learn to Swim. BFA Educational Media, 2211 Michigan Avenue, Santa Monica, California 90404. These two captioned filmstrips follow a young boy and girl from their first swimming class through their development and accomplishment in the sport.

Multi-Media Reading Skill Kits. Troll Associates, 320 Route 17, Mahwah, New Jersey 07430. A new series with each kit composed of a short book containing information about an aspect of the sport (football—the kicking game), a cassette tape that follows the book, a filmstrip that is based upon the book and synchronized with the cassette and activity skill cards that can be used for follow-up reinforcement. This kit is clearly one of the finest products on the market.

New Sports Techniques. Super 8mm Cassette and 16mm Reel to Reel, Athletic Institute, 705 Merchandise Mart, Chicago, Illinois 60654. A new series of film loops (1976) in minor (soccer) and lifetime sports (golf, badminton). These, longer than most film loops (13–20 minutes) are still useful for self-instruction in the library and as a stimulus to reading.

Sports Close-ups. Mankato, Minnesota: Crestwood House, 1975/76. A series of multimedia kits on series sports heroes. Each kit contains a soft cover book and a read along cassette. This kit will be especially appealing to some youngsters as it gives insights into the off-the-field activities of the stars as well as helping the reluctant and slow reader to read.

Sports Superstars. Mankato, Minnesota: Creative Education, 1974. A series of books with accompanying cassette that follows the text word by word. The series is more advanced than comparable book-cassette kits and as such, would be for the intermediate level student who has established some skill in reading. Examples of titles in the series are: *Hank Aaron, Jack Nicklaus, Peggy Fleming,* and *Poncho Gonzales*.

Women Who Win. EMC Corporation, 1974. A new series that combines a cassette tape with a short booklet on famous women athletes (Chris Evert, Janet Lynn). This series will be extremely valuable to the reluctant reader.

Bulletin Board Materials

Converse 1976 Basketball Yearbook. Converse, Wilmington, Massachusetts 01887. A collection of statistics, information, and pictures from the previous season. The annual contains highlights on professional, college, and high school teams as well as sports trivia (miles traveled for certain teams) and interesting anecdotes on basketball oddities. Several items can be cut out and posted to attract interest to a book display.

For Your Bulletin Board. Pennsylvania Athletic Products Division, The General Tire and Rubber Company, Box 951, Akron, Ohio, 43309. A series of bulletin board materials in several sports with pictures of players performing certain techniques. Captions explain each technique. One or two of these can be used to catch interest on a bulletin board.

Fundamentals for Better Basketball. Converse. A short booklet containing suggestions for self-improvement of the basketball player. Illustrations demonstrate technique as an eye-catcher for bulletin boards.

Let's Look at Sports Chart Series. Instructor. A series of $11\frac{1}{2}''$ × $16''$ charts covering 24 sports that describe the equipment, terminology, history and action of each sport. For each, there are six charts, in addition to information photos and diagrams.

Pictures. College and professional teams will provide pictures in black and white by request. These are both head and action shots that make excellent bulletin board of display materials, especially when coordinated with a book about the athlete.

Press Books. Most colleges and professional teams make available to the public press books. In some cases, there is a charge but in most, they are provided gratis. These contain pictures and can be used in bulletin board or other displays. The professional teams also sell team yearbooks, which also contain fine bulletin board materials.

Exposé and Protest

Bouton, Jim. *I'm Glad You Didn't Take It Personally.* Morrow, 1971. Bouton, the author of *Ball Four,* a book critical of baseball, tells of the reactions to his first book as well as his attempt to make a comeback as a player.

Edwards, Harry. *The Revolt of the Black Athlete.* The Free Press, 1969. The author, active in the Black athlete's movement, has detailed the historical and contemporary involvement of Blacks in sports. Specifically, he criticizes the misuse of Black athletes in college and the pro's and the blatant racism in sports at all levels.

Hoch, Paul. *Rip Off the Big Game: The Exploitation of Sports by the Power Elite.* Anchor Books, 1972. He analyzes the present state of big time/big business sports and finds it lacking in many areas. Hoch criticizes the dehumanizing aspects of athletics, and preoccupation of owners with making money, the conformity and blind obedience required of players, sexist attitudes, and racial discrimination.

Meggyesy, Dave. *I Was Playing for Survival.* Ramparts Press, 1970. The fascinating rags-to-riches story of a successful player who questions the system and the tactics of football coaches. The author recounts the price he paid to be successful and wonders if it was worth it.

Olsen, Jack. *The Black Athlete: A Shameful Story.* Time-Life, 1968. Because of the recent changes in society and sports, this book is somewhat dated. However, it still contains a wealth of information from the experiences of Black athletes involving discrimination in sports.

Sample, Johnny, with Fred Hamilton and Sonny Schwartz. *Confessions of a Dirty Ballplayer.* Dell, 1970. An autobiographic account that attempts to look inside football. Considered to be of protest-exposé variety of sports literature, it is not quite as radical as most in this category.

Summary

In 1923, Ellwood Cubberley encouraged principals to provide for flexibility in the curriculum: "even in schools where the courses of study is rigidly outlined, and even based on definite page assignments in definite textbooks, the principal will still find it possible to suggest some points for omission or emphasis."[1] Fortunately, today's educators have a wide range of methods, strategies, and curricular arrangements available and have the freedom to use them.

Clearly one of the most useful and educationally sound curriculum revisions that has appeared on the scene is the simple restructuring of the length of courses. This results in a flexible and comprehensive program called minicourses. Defined as "any educational experience that involves a detailed and in-depth study of a specific unit or subject, jointly planned by student and teacher, and for which less than a semester of time is used,"[2] this grass roots movement has several clear advantages that require the serious concern of all educators.

While characterization is difficult because of the individual and local nature of the movement, the following are the general advantages:

a. The program has great appeal to students and they find it interesting and relevant; it has led to a revitalization of English and the social studies.

b. Students have a more positive attitude toward the course than do students in a traditional arrangement.

c. Students have a more positive attitude toward the teacher than do students in a traditional arrangement.

d. Teachers have a more positive attitude toward their students and the teaching profession than do teachers instructing traditional courses.

97

e. In most situations attendance has increased during the period of the program.

f. The courses capitalize on the interests and strengths of the teachers.

g. Promotion of mutual cooperation between the school and community; this can lead to improved school-community relationships.

h. Students have opportunities to develop responsibility through aiding in the planning, co-teaching and coordinating of the program.

i. The program promotes humanistic education in large schools which are sometimes impersonal.

j. The program seems to offer students in small schools more content and opportunity for in-depth enrichment than ordinarily available.

k. Minicourse arrangements encourage interdisciplinary offerings and interdisciplinary learning experiences.

l. The opportunity for promoting affective education through student involvement and the arrangement of options within the system characterizes mini's.

m. Students benefit from the learning experiences associated with minicourses that emphasize action (field trips, simulations, demonstrations) and de-emphasize textbook approaches.

n. Mini's offer provision for individual differences.

o. Because of the heterogeneous grouping arrangements of students the stigma usually attached to students in slower sections is diminished.

p. The inexpensive nature of mini's (normally just a small sum in the school budget) helps to encourage their development and use by the school administration and school board.

q. The program meets the challenge of change within the system through student, teacher, and administrative cooperative planning that bears results.

r. The flexibility of the mini arrangement permits the curriculum to meet the needs of the student whether cognitive, affective, or psychomotor. If a needs analysis survey reveals the lack of job awareness, a mini can satisfy this more quickly than through traditional curriculum integration procedures.

s. Significant possibilities exist for the development of self-esteem among students. For the problem student mini's offer a real chance for a fresh start—a chance to get back in the game.

t. Teachers and students have the opportunity to meet and share common interests not normally found in the conventional setting.

u. Mini's advance a feeling of electricity and enthusiasm that carries over to the entire school program.[3]

The disadvantages though fortunately few do exist and their avoidance will significantly improve the success of the program.

    a. Scheduling difficulties generally arise; matching students to offerings through computer assistance helps avoid this snag.

    b. The assignment of a mini to teachers lacking proper background can cause problems. Hopefully, this book offers guidelines to aid teachers in this situation.

    c. Instructors may try to incorporate too much information into a mini resulting in a miseducational experience.

    d. Research and evaluation of programs has been minimal. This seems to be quickly changing with even some doctoral thesis' completed in the area. Each school's own program evaluation will furnish accountability documentation for the community and permit modifications where needed.

    e. Poor planning, lack of in-depth intellectually honest treatment and conventional traditional approaches but with exotic new titles (old wine, new bottle) have characterized some courses. Using a systematic approach, these problems can easily be avoided.

    f. Inadequate coverage of basic curricular areas can result in graduates with serious knowledge and skill weaknesses in critical subjects. The avoidance of this disadvantage through guided selection, faculty advisement of students, and process-skills emphasis will result in a more productive and profitable program.[4]

The removal of these disadvantages, while not guaranteeing success, will significantly contribute to the realization of the potential of the minicourse program.

The concept of short intensive courses while new to education has successfully served as part of the training programs of business, government, and the military for many years. This refreshing alternative can stimulate educators and students to make learning rewarding and satisfying, consequently enabling students not only to acquire knowledge but to enjoy its acquisition. Few, if any, educational innovations can point to such successful claims backed by research. If the critics of education are correct in their criticism that the school curriculum is irrelevant, impersonal, and outdated, then minicourses hold the key to changing that situation.

References

Chapter Two—Why Minicourses?

1. Oliver, Albert. *Curriculum Improvement, A Guide to Problems, Principles, and Procedures.* New York: Dodd, Mead and Company, 1974. p. 22.
2. Roberts, Arthur D. and Robert K. Gable. "The Minicourse: Where the Affective and Cognitive Meet." *Phi Delta Kappan.* May 1973. Vol. 54.
3. One of the threats to the validity of research studies on minicourses is innovation effect. That is, positive results may occur because of the new approach rather than because of the program.
4. Kohut, Sylvester. "Mini-Courses in the High School Social Studies Curriculum." *The Social Studies.* April 1973. Vol. 64. No. 4. p. 170; and Sylvester Kohut, "A Comparison of Student Achievement and Retention on Subjective Versus Objective Examinations in the Social Studies as Influenced by Different Instructional Patterns," unpublished Doctoral Dissertation, The Pennsylvania State University, 1971.
5. Gudaitis, Donald. "Minicourses: Are They Useful?" *The Clearing House.* April 1972. Vol. 46. pp. 465–7.
6. Hayward, Robert R. "Maximum Results from Mini-Courses." *Today's Education.* September, 1969. Vol. 58. p. 56.
7. *Ibid.*
8. *Ibid.*, p. 57.
9. *Ibid.*
10. Roberts, Arthur D. and Robert K. Gable, p. 622.
11. If the minicourse program takes as its methodological strategy a process approach working toward discovering the structure of a discipline, this segmented approach need not be a problem. See Jerome Bruner, *The Process of Education.* Cambridge, Massachusetts: Howard University Press, 1960; and Barry Beyer, *Inquiry in the Social Studies Classroom. A Strategy for Teaching.* Columbus, Ohio: Charles Merrill Publishing Company, 1971.
12. *Ibid.* p. 56.
13. Glatthorn, Allan A. *Alternatives in Education: Schools and Programs.* New York: Dodd, Mead and Company, 1975. pp. 104–5.

Chapter Three—Systematic Development

1. Roberts, Arthur D. and Robert K. Gable. p. 623.
2. Hayward, Robert R., p. 56.
3. Stern, Adele H. "Sorry Dr. Silberman! Mini-courses in the High School." *English Journal.* April 1972. Vol. 61. pp. 552.
4. Glatthorn, Allan. p. 92.
5. Swenson, William G. *Guide to Minicourse/Electives Programs.* New York: Bantam Books, 1972. p. 7.
6. "Flirting with Free Forming." *Nation's Schools.* July 1972. Vol. 90. p. 25.
7. Glatthorn, Allan. p. 92.

8. Roberts, Arthur D. and Robert K. Gable. p. 622.
9. Parkinson, Daniel S. "The Minicourse Approach in Ohio." *Phi Delta Kappan*. April 1976. Vol. 57. p. 552.
10. Guenther, John and Robert Ridgeway. "Mini-Courses: One Way To Provide More Humanistic School Programs." *NASSP Bulletin*. April 1976. Vol. 60. p. 14.
11. Wilson, Robert E. *Educational Administration*. Columbus, Ohio: Charles E. Merrill Publishing Company, 1966. p. 481.
12. Gudaitis, Donald. p. 465.
13. Roberts, Arthur D. and Robert K. Gable. p. 622.
14. Parkinson, Daniel S. p. 551.
15. In a doctoral dissertation, Anderson and Kubicek found: "Minicourses generally require more of the instructor's time for organization, field trips, and evaluation." Jack Ron Anderson and Leonard Kubicek. *The Development and Affective Evaluation of a Minicourse Structure for General Education Earth Science*. Doctoral Dissertation, University of Northern Colorado, 1973.
16. Mager, Robert. *Preparing Instructional Objectives*. Belmont, California: Fearon Publishers, 1962.
17. DeCecco, John P. and William R. Crawford. *The Psychology of Learning and Instruction: Educational Psychology*. Englewood Cliffs, New Jersey: Prentice-Hall, 1968. pp. 238–476.
18. Russell, James. *Modular Instruction*. Minneapolis: Burgess Publishing Company, 1974. p. 41.
19. Parkinson, Daniel S. p. 552.
20. Heitzmann, Wm. Ray. *Educational Games and Simulations*. Washington, D.C.: National Educational Education Association, 1974. pp. 18–19.
21. Charles, C. M. *Individualized Instruction*. St. Louis: The C. V. Mosby Company, 1976.
22. Engel, R. A. and L. D. Weller, Jr. "Mini-Courses: Maxi-Morale." *High School Journal*. December 1972. Vol. 56. p. 146.
23. Glatthorn, Allan A. p. 115.
24. "Back to Basics in the Schools." *Newsweek*. October 21, 1974; and Suzanne DeLesseps, "Education's Return To Basics." *Editorial Research Reports*. September 12, 1975. Vol. 2. No. 10.
25. Gerlach, Vernon S. and Donald P. Ely. *Teaching and Media: A Systematic Approach*. Englewood Cliffs, New Jersey: Prentice-Hall, 1971. p. 17.
26. Schmuck, Richard A. and Patricia A. Schmuck. *Group Processes in the Classroom*. Dubuque, Iowa: Wm. C. Brown, 1975. pp. 1, 3, 4.
27. Ibid. p. 191.
28. Weise, Charles. "Mini-Courses: New Spark for Student Enrichment." *Nation's Schools*. May, 1970. vol. 85. p. 74.
29. "Flirting with Free Forming." p. 26.
30. Steirer, Michael D. "Minicourses Get It All In." *School Shop*. October 1974. Vol. 34. p. 65.
31. Hayward, Robert R., p. 56.
32. Parkinson, Daniel S. p. 552.
33. Dale, Edgar. *Audio-Visual Methods in Teaching*. New York: Holt, Rinehart and Winston, 1969.

34. In addition to surveying other districts and other schools for mini-course outlines and materials, two other sources may help: the states' Departments of Education and *Resources in Education* (*Research in Education* prior to 1975), which lists information and courses which can be obtained through the ERIC system.

35. Swenson, William G. p. 7.

36. TenBrink, Terry D. *Evaluation: A Practical Guide for Teachers.* New York: McGraw-Hill Book Company, 1974. pp. 114–115.

37. Heitzmann, Wm. Ray and Charles Staropoli. "The Social Studies Teacher and Measuring the Affect of Classroom Instruction." *The Social Studies Journal.* Spring 1974. Vol. 3. No. 4.

38. Krathwohl, David R., Benjamin S. Bloom and Bertram B. Masia. *Taxonomy of Educational Objectives—Handbook II: The Affective Domain.* New York: Longmans, Green, 1964.

39. Bloom, Benjamin S. *Taxonomy of Educational Objectives—Handbook I: The Cognitive Domain.* New York: Longmans, Green, 1956.

40. Kibler, Robert J., Larry L. Barker and David Miles. *Behavioral Objectives and Instruction.* Boston: Allyn and Bacon, 1970. pp. 68–75.

Chapter Four—Studying Others' Minicourses

1. Harris, Louis. "Crisis in the High Schools: The Life Poll." *Life.* May 16, 1969. Vol. 66. No. 19. p. 31.

Chapter Five—Minicourse 1: "America's Maritime Heritage"

1. Heitzmann, Wm. Ray. "America's Forgotten Maritime Heritage: A Bicentennial Treasure. *Social Education.* October, 1976. Vol. 40. No. 1.

2. Batchelder, Samuel F. "Some Sea Terms in Land Speech." *New England Quarterly.* October 1929. Vol. 2. pp. 625–653.

3. Calkins, Lieutenant Carlos, U.S.N. "Historical and Professional Notes on the Naval Campaign of Manila Bay in 1898." *United States Naval Institute Proceedings.* June, 1899. Vol. 25. pp. 267–322; and Admiral Dewey *United States Naval Institute Proceedings.* September, 1899.

Chapter Six—Minicourse 2: "Sports Literature"

1. Arbuthnot, May Hill and Zena Sutherland. *Children and Books.* Glenview, Illinois: Scott, Foresman and Company, 1972. p. 471.

2. Heitzmann, Kathleen and Wm. Ray Heitzmann. "The Athletic Coach and the Library." *Illinois Libraries.* March, 1972. Vol. 54. No. 3. pp. 226–7.

3. Coach Sanford Patlak of the University of Chicago Laboratory High School, a pioneer in aiding students through the use of sports literature, states his views: "I'm out after those in trouble in reading. . . . When I find someone who likes sports but dislikes reading, I pick up the ball. Catch such students early; you may be able to change their attitude toward books—help prevent discouragement, failure, even their dropping out of school." Ellen Lamar Thomas. "Books are the Greatest." *Journal of Reading.* November, 1968. Haywood Dotson, former basketball star at Columbia University, gives the

students' point of view: "I read everything our (Junior High School) library had on basketball, but it's funny, the book that did the most for me was a dinky, little publication called *How to Star in Basketball*. It was the first one I read. I must have gone through it five or six times. Just basic stuff, but it was all valuable—how to change direction, how to move without the ball, how to shoot the jump shot, etc. For example, I'd had my elbow out when I shot the jumper, and the book said 'elbow in.' Everybody else developed his own (jumper), but I did things by the book." Haywood Dotson. *Scholastic Coach*. May, 1968.

Summary

1. Cubberley, Ellwood. *The Principal and His School*. Boston: Houghton Mifflin Company, 1923. pp. 388–389.
2. Loar, Robert L. "Zap—You're Sterile," National Association of Secondary School Principals Annual Convention, March 1–6, 1974, Atlantic City. *Research in Education*. Vol. 9. No. 12. December, 1974. ED 094 452.
3. Guenther, John and Robert Ridgeway, pp. 13–14. William G. Kerr. *A Study of Designated Affective Behaviors of High School Students Enrolled in Mini-courses and Traditional Courses*, Doctoral Dissertation. Wayne State University, 1975. Albert Oliver. "Maximizing the Mini: A Look at Curriculum Alternatives." National Association of Secondary School Principals Annual Convention, March 1–6, 1974. *Research in Education*. Vol. 9. No. 8. August, 1974. ED 089 441. Patricia Huwa. "Quarter System Biology in a Small School." *The American Biology Teacher*. February, 1973. Vol. 35. p. 96. Marjorie Gardner. "Modules and Minicourses for the Integrated Sciences." *The Science Teacher*. February, 1973. Vol 40. p. 31. Jack Ron Anderson and Leonard Kubicek. *The Development and Effective Evaluation of a Minicourse Structure for General Education Earth Science*, Doctoral Dissertation. University of Northern Colorado, 1973. Arthur D. Roberts and Robert K. Gable. "Mini Versus Traditional: An Experimental Study of High School Social Studies Curricula." National Council for the Social Studies Annual Meeting, November, 1972. Boston. *Research in Education*. September, 1973. Vol. 8. No. 9. ED 076 471. Edward Tresnak. *A Study of the Use of Short Courses in Illinois Public High Schools With Emphasis on Factors Which Lead to the Success or Failure of Short Course Plans*, Doctoral Dissertation. Northern Illinois University, 1973.
4. Roberts, Arthur D. and Robert K. Gable. "The Minicourse: Where the Affective and Cognitive Meet," p. 623. Edward Tresnak. Robert Hayward, p. 56.

Bibliography

Minicourses

Anderson, Jack Ron, and Leonard Kubicek. *The Development and Affective Evaluation of a Minicourse Structure for General Education Earth Science*, Doctoral Dissertation. University of Northern Colorado, 1973.

Bancroft, M. A. "Scheduling for Elective Courses," *School and Community*, Vol. 61, January, 1975.

Barbour, G. C. "Teaching English in Small Doses; Mt. Pleasant High School." *Pennsylvania School Journal*, Vol. 121, February, 1973.

Barrow, Joseph and John W. Lakus. "Minicourses—New Program Features Student Self-Selection," *The Science Teacher*. Vol. 39, May, 1972.

Beers, R. B. "Use of Activity-Centered Minicourses to Solve Difficult Educational Problems," *School Teacher*, Vol. 40, September, 1973.

"Best Activity Program May Be Mini-Courses During the School Day," *The Education Summary*. February 18, 1972.

Bicknell, John E., et al. "Microteaching and the Minicourse: A Brief Overview of the Programs of the Far West Laboratory," State University of New York, Fredonia College at Fredonia, 1970. *Research in Education*, Vol. 6, No. 7, July, 1971. ED 049 163.

Bischak, Walter A. *An Examination of the Mini-Course Program at Westfield High School*, Master's Thesis. Jersey City State College, 1972.

Blake, Norman. *Curriculum Change in a Small High School Conversion From a 'Traditional' to a 'Short Course' Curriculum. The Historical Development of the 'Small-Way' 'Micro-Course' Curriculum Project 150 at Iowa Valley High School*, Marengo, Iowa, Master's Thesis. Drake University, 1975.

Boccia, Robert M. *Mini-Course for the Non-Business High School Student at Bristol Eastern High School*, Master's Thesis. Central Connecticut State College, 1975.

Borg, Walter R. "Guidelines for the Development of Minicourses," Far West Lab. for Educational Research and Development. Berkeley, California. *Research in Education*, Vol. 6, No. 11, November, 1971, ED 053 091.

Caffyn, Lois. "Nongraded Quarter Selectives: Mini-Guidelines for Mini-Courses," Kansas State Department of Education, Topeka, Kansas, 1972. *Research in Education*, Vol. 8, No. 6, June, 1973. ED 072 438.

Cross, P. C. "Choice Can Be Too Much," *Scholastic Review*, Vol. 78, February, 1970.

DesChamps, William Bert. "*A Case History of the Development and Implementation of the Nine-Week Course Concept at Besser Junion High School in Alpena, Michigan,*" Doctoral Dissertation. Michigan State University, 1972.

Dupuis, V. L. "Shake-Up the Curriculum: Mini-Course Preparation." *NASSP Bulletin*, Vol. 59. September, 1975.

Engel, R. A., and L. D. Weller, Jr. "Mini-Courses: Maxi-Morale," *High School Journal*. Vol. 56, December, 1972.

Experiment in Free-Form Education: Mini-Courses" *ERS Information Aid*. October, 1970. No. 6

Fenwick, J. J. "Mini-Course Curriculum." *NASSP Bulletin*, Vol. 54. February, 1970.

Fontana, C. J. "Speech Communication Minicourses in a High School Language Arts Department." *The Speech Teacher*. Vol. 23. March 1974.

"Foreign Language Option: The Mini-Course." *Curriculum Report* (NASSP) October, 1973 Vol. 3, No. 1

Gardner, Marjorie. "Modules and Minicourses in a High School Language Arts Department." *The Speech Teacher*. Vol. 23, March, 1974.

Grasso, R. "Content vs. Creativity vs. Time: A Solution." *The American Biology Teacher*. Vol. 32. October, 1972.

Gudaitis, Donald J. "Mini Courses: Are They Useful?" *The Clearing House*. Vol. 46. April, 1972.

Guenther, John. "More Humanistic Social Studies Programs Through Mini-Courses," 1975. *Research in Education*, Vol. 11. No. 4, April, 1976, ED 115 571.

Guenther, J., and R. Ridgeway, "Mini-Courses: One Way to Provide More Humanistic School Programs." *NASSP Bulletin*. Vol. 60, April, 1976.

Guenther, J., and R. Ridgeway, "Mini-Courses: Promising Alternative in the Social Studies." *The Clearing House*, Vol. 47, April, 1973.

Hayward, Robert R. "Maximum Results From Mini-Courses." *Today's Education*. Vol. 58, 1969.

Huwa, Patricia. "Quarter-System Biology in a Small High School." *The American Biology Teacher*, Vol. 35, February, 1973.

Kerr, William Gordon. *A Study of Designated Affective Behaviors of High School Students Enrolled in Minicourses and Traditional Courses*, Doctoral Dissertation. Wayne State University, 1975.

Kohut, Sylvester, Jr. "Mini-Courses in the High School Social Studies Curriculum." *The Social Studies*. Vol. 64, April, 1973.

Lee, J. P., and J. C. March, "Time Utilization for Optimum Learning." *The Journal of Secondary Education*. Vol. 44, February, 1969.

Loar, Robert L. "Zap—You're Sterile." March, 1974. *Research in Education*. Vol. 9. No. 12, December, 1974. ED 094 452.

Maase, E. "My Daughter and the English Department; or, A Second-Hand Look at High School Mini-Courses." *English Journal*. Vol. 63, April, 1974.

"Maxi List of Minicourse Ideas; New Trier East High School, Winnetka, Illinois," *Nation's Schools*, Vol. 93, March, 1974.

Means, R. Don. "Mini Course Directory." Clarion State College, Pennsylvania Council on Year-Round Education; Pennsylvania State Department of Education, 1973. *Research in Education*, Vol. 9. No. 2, February, 1974. ED 082 295.

Myers, Kent C. "Instructional Balance: A Goal." *Phi Delta Kappan*. Vol. 55. June, 1974.

NEA Research Division. "Free-Form Education; Mini-Courses or Elective Units." *NEA Research Bulletin*. Vol. 50, May, 1972.

Oliver, Albert I. "Maximizing the Mini: A Look at Curriculum Alternatives." March, 1974. *Research in Education*. Vol. 9, No. 8, August, 1974. ED 089 441.

Parkinson, D. S. "The Minicourse Approach in Ohio." *Phi Delta Kappan*. Vol. 57. April, 1976.

Pepe, Thomas J. "Something Special: Enrichment Courses at Very Little Extra Cost." *School Management*. Vol. 17, April, 1973.

Pittsburgh Board of Public Education. "English Mini-Course Journalism (Preliminary, Unedited Version.)." September, 1971. *Research in Education*. Vol. 8. No. 5 May, 1973. ED 071 085.

Pittsburgh Board of Public Education. "English Mini-Course World Literature (Preliminary, Unedited Version.)." December, 1971. *Research in Education*. Vol. 8. No. 5. May, 1973. ED 071 086.

Postlethwait, S. N. "Time for Microcourses?" *The Library College Journal*. Vol. 2. No. 2. Winter, 1969.

Postlethwait, S. N., and Frank Mercer. "Minicourses—What Are They?" Purdue Research Foundation. Lafayette, Indiana, 1972. *Research in Education*. Vol. 9 No. 11. November, 1974. ED 093 654.

"Principals Tell Pro's, Con's of Short Courses." *NASSP Spotlight*. April, 1974.

Roberts, A. D., and R. K. Gable. "Minicourses: Where the Affective and Cognitive Meet." *Phi Delta Kappan*. Vol. 54. May, 1973.

Roberts, A.D., and R. K. Gable. "Mini Versus Traditional: An Experimental Study of High School Social Studies Curricula." November, 1972. *Research in Education*. Vol. 8, No. 9. September, 1973. ED 076 471.

Russell, James D. *Modular Instruction*. Minneapolis: Burgess Publishing Company, 1974.

Seretny, Albert A. "Yale-New Haven History Education Project (H.E.P.). Summary Report 1970–1973. (And) Guide for Mini-Course Teachers." New Haven Public Schools and Yale University, Connecticut, 1972. *Research in Education*. Vol. 9. No. 8. August, 1974. ED 090 091.

"Schools Find Mini-Courses Have Maxi-Popularity." *Education Summary*. December 18, 1970.

Steirer, M. D. "Mini-Courses Get It All In." *School Shop*. Vol. 34. October, 1974.

Stern, Adele H. "Sorry Dr. Silberman! Minicourses in the High School." *English Journal*. Vol. 61. April, 1972.

Swenson, William G. *Guide to Minicourse/Electives Programs*. New York: Bantam Books, 1972.

Tresnak, Edward H. *A Study of the Use of Short Courses in Illinois Public High Schools with Emphasis on Factors Which Lead to the Success or Failure of Short Course Plans*, Doctoral Dissertation. Northern Illinois University, 1973.

Webb, B. G. "Student-Taught Mini-Courses." *School and Community*. Vol. 60, January, 1974.

Wiese, Charles R. "Mini Courses: New Spark for Student Enrichment." *Nation's Schools*. Vol. 85. May, 1970.

Youngren, Robert. "For a Change of Pace, Try a Mini-Course Day." *The Clearing House*. Vol. 47. November, 1972.

Curriculum, Instruction and Evaluation

Alexander, William M., Galen J. Saylor and Emmett Williams. *The High School: Today and Tomorrow*. New York: Holt, Rinehart and Winston, Inc., 1971.

Arnoult, Malcolm D. *Fundamentals of Scientific Method in Psychology*. 2d ed. Dubuque, Iowa: Wm. C. Brown Company Publishers, 1976.

Bloom, Benjamin S., Thomas J. Hastings and George F. Madaus. *Handbook on Formative and Summative Evaluation of Student Learning*. New York: McGraw-Hill Book Company, 1971.

Brophy, Jere E. and Thomas L. Good. *Teacher-Student Relationships: Causes and Consequences*. New York: Holt, Rinehart and Winston, Inc., 1974.

Carin, Arthur A. and Robert B. Sund. *Developing Questioning Techniques: A Self-Concept Approach*. Columbus, Ohio: Charles E. Merrill Publishing Company, 1971.

Chapin, June R. and Richard E. Gross. *Teaching Social Studies Skills*. Boston: Little, Brown and Company, 1973.

Charles, C. M. *Individualized Instruction*. Saint Louis: The C. V. Mosby Company, 1976.

Clark, Leonard H. and Irving S. Starr. *Secondary School Teaching Methods*. 3d ed. New York: Macmillan Publishing Co., Inc., 1976.

DeCecco, John P. and William R. Crawford. *The Psychology of Learning and Instruction: Educational Psychology*. Englewood Cliffs, New Jersey: Prentice-Hall, Inc., 1974.

Dunfee, Maxine (ed.). *Eliminating Ethnic Bias in Instructional Materials: Comment and Bibliography*. Washington, D.C.: Association for Supervision and Curriculum Development, 1974.

Gaddis, Edwin A. *Teaching the Slow Learner in the Regular Classroom*. Belmont, California: Fearon Publishers, 1971.

Gagne, Robert M. and Leslie J. Briggs. *Principles of Instructional Design*. New York: Holt, Rinehart and Winston, Inc., 1974.

Gerlach, Vernon S. and Donald P. Ely. *Teaching and Media: A Systematic Approach*. Englewood Cliffs, New Jersey: Prentice-Hall, Inc., 1971.

Glatthorn, Allan A. *Alternatives in Education: Schools and Programs*. New York: Dodd, Mead & Company, 1975.

Good, Thomas L., Bruce Biddle and Jere E. Brophy. *Teachers Make a Difference*. New York: Holt, Rinehart and Winston, 1975.

Grambs, Jean D., John Carr and Robert M. Fitch. *Modern Methods in Secondary Education*. 3d ed. New York: Holt, Rinehart and Winston, Inc., 1970.

Gray, Jenny. *Teacher's Survival Guide.* Belmont, California: Fearon Publishers, 1967.

Gronlund, Norman E. *Measurement and Evaluation in Teaching.* 3d ed. New York: Macmillan Publishing Co., Inc., 1976.

Hamilton, Norman K. and Galen J. Saylor. *Humanizing the Secondary School.* Washington, D.C.: Association for Supervision and Curriculum Development, NEA, 1969.

Haney, John B. and Eldon J. Ullmer. *Educational Media and the Teacher.* Dubuque, Iowa: Wm. C. Brown Company, 1970.

Heitzmann, Wm. Ray, *Educational Games and Simulations.* Washington, D.C.: National Education Association, 1974.

Hoover, Kenneth H. *Learning and Teaching in the Secondary School: Improved Instructional Practices.* 3d ed. Boston: Allyn and Bacon, Inc., 1972.

Hyman, Ronald T. (ed.). *Contemporary Thought on Teaching.* Englewood Cliffs, New Jersey: Prentice-Hall, Inc., 1970.

Inlow, Gail M. *Maturity in High School Teaching.* 2nd ed. Englewood Cliffs, New Jersey: Prentice-Hall, Inc., 1970.

Karlin, Muriel Schoenbrun and Regina Berger. *The Effective Student Activities Program.* West Nyack, N.Y.: Parker Publishing Company, Inc.—Englewood Cliffs, New Jersey: Prentice-Hall, Inc., 1971.

Kemp, Jerrold E. *Planning and Producing Audiovisual Materials.* New York: Chandler Publishing Company, 1968.

Kibler, Robert J., Larry L. Barker and David T. Miles. *Behavioral Objectives and Instruction.* Boston: Allyn and Bacon, Inc., 1970.

Kinder, James S. *Using Instructional Media.* New York: D. Van Nostrand Company, 1973.

Kryspin, William J. and John F. Feldhusen. *Developing Classroom Tests: A Guide for Writing and Evaluating Test Items.* Minneapolis: Burgess Publishing Company, 1974.

Leeper, Robert R. (ed.). *Strategy for Curriculum Change.* (ASCD Seminar on Strategy for Curriculum Change: Proceedings) Washington, D.C.: Association for Supervision and Curriculum Development, 1965.

Leonard, Leo D. and Robert T. Utz. *Building Skills for Competency-Based Teaching.* New York: Harper and Row, Publishers, 1974.

Logan, Frank A. *Fundamentals of Learning and Motivation.* Second edition. Dubuque, Iowa: Wm. C. Brown Company Publishers, 1976.

Mager, Robert F. *Developing Attitude Toward Learning.* Belmont, California: Fearon Publishers, 1968.

Minor, E. O. and Harvey R. Frye. *Techniques for Producing Visual Instructional Media.* New York: McGraw-Hill Book Company, 1969.

Nations, Jimmy E. *Learning Centers in the Classroom.* Washington, D.C.: National Education Association, 1976.

Overly, Norman V. (ed.) *The Unstudied Curriculum: Its Impact on Children.* Washington, D.C.: Association for Supervision and Curriculum Development, NEA, 1970.

Palardy, J. Michael. *Teaching Today: Tasks and Challenges.* New York: Macmillan Publishing Company, Inc. 1974.

Payne, David A. *The Assessment of Learning: Cognitive and Affective.* Lexington, Massachusetts: D. C. Heath and Company, 1974.

Ringness, Thomas A. *The Affective Domain in Education.* Boston: Little, Brown and Company, 1975.

Roe, William H. and Thelbert L. Drake. *Principalship.* New York: Macmillan Publishing Co., Inc., 1974.

Schmuch, Richard A. and Patricia Schmuck. *Group Processes in the Classroom.* 2nd ed. Dubuque, Iowa: Wm. C. Brown Company Publishers, 1975.

Skeel, Dorothy J. (ed.). *The Challenge of Teaching Social Studies in the Elementary School: Readings.* Pacific Palisades, California: Goodyear Publishing Company, Inc., 1970.

Smith, Fred M. and Sam Adams. *Educational Measurement for the Classroom Teacher.* New York: Harper & Row Publishers, 1972.

TenBrink, Terry D. *Evaluation: A Practical Guide for Teachers.* New York: McGraw-Hill Book Company, 1974.

Thomas, George and Joseph Crescimbani. *Guiding the Gifted Child.* Philadelphia: Philadelphia Book Company, Inc.

Trow, William Clark. *Teacher and Technology: New Designs for Learning.* New York: Appleton-Century-Crofts—Englewood Cliffs, New Jersey: Prentice Hall, Inc., 1963.

Unruh, Glenys G. and William M. Alexander. *Innovations in Secondary Education.* 2nd ed. New York: Holt, Rinehart and Winston, Inc., 1974.

Appendices

Appendix A
Successful Free Forming: Checklist for Schools

Want to avoid problems that make free forming more fiasco than fiesta? Then look to the list below. It covers some tips for getting around major problems successfully.

Make sure you communicate free form's educational goals to your community, especially parent groups. Otherwise, citizens may criticize it as an "odd-ball experiment" and a waste of tax money. One way to communicate: Prepare written materials to distribute at PTA meetings. New Trier East High School, Winnetka, Illinois, offered parents a 10-point rationale that spelled out benefits the school hopes to achieve, *e.g.* "Students and teachers will become increasingly aware that the community is rich in human resources which should be tapped by schools."

Let teachers know right from the beginning that you'll welcome their participation as both planners and instructors. Don't be surprised if some teachers are initially lukewarm to free forming. Experience shows most teachers come around, once they see others involved.

Emphasizing that students should be accommodated first, allow teachers to register for courses they'd like to take. Just as students learn from playing teacher, the faculty can benefit from playing student.

If controversial speakers or activities are on the agenda, keep publicity about them in perspective. Don't make a point about playing them up because sensational press coverage only antagonizes a lot of people. If they do get blown up locally, emphasize that they are only part of a much larger program.

Make sure the board knows about the free form program ahead of time. Send them a copy of the schedule at least two to three weeks in advance. That way, they'll be prepared to handle any questions—or flak—from the public.

Since student interest and participation is all-important, be sure to go to youngsters for suggestions on program content. If you plan to use polls, learn a lesson from New Trier: Ask students to specify course titles.

From *Nation's Schools,* Volume 90, Number 1, July 1972. Copyright © 1972 by McGraw-Hill, Inc. Reprinted with permission.

If planning to register students, get schedules out two to three weeks early so they have time to study and make choices carefully. Since youngsters object strongly to being herded into a dining hall or auditorium all together, consider asking teachers to serve as registrars for groups of 10 to 20 students.

Brief teachers on the content of the program, so that they can answer students' questions about it. That will cut down on students coming to the office for information.

Post schedules of the program around the school the day it begins. Otherwise students will be pouring into the office trying to remember where they should be going at what time.

Allow enough time between registration and program date to handle any rescheduling that may be necessary, *e.g.* adding extra sections to a popular mini, moving a course or activity to a larger room to accommodate more students. At least a week is advisable.

Ask student volunteers or the typing classes to help get out letters to resource people.

Schedule free forming at the end of the week so everyone has a chance to recover over a weekend. A time favored by schools seems to be the doldrum period in February, March or April when routine needs a good sparking.

To make the most of field trips, allot time beforehand to prep youngsters on the places or events they'll be seeing. When they return, set aside time for them to discuss their experiences and share impressions.

Keep in mind free forming offers an opportunity to experiment with new teaching styles as well as new content. Major criticism of most free forming has been that its programs remain too closely tied to the public school idiom, despite the fact that they're generally more interesting to the kids. Encourage teachers to try out methods others than "chalk and talk."

Don't forget to evaluate carefully when the program is over. Ask all participants for solid criticism and suggestions for improvement.

If the program isn't covered by the media, write up a story for the local newspaper and send out a special report to the community to fill them in.

Appendix B
Abridged List of Minicourses Offered at Washington Senior High School, Sioux Falls, South Dakota

Learn to Drive the Stick Shift
The Feel of Communication:
  Emphasis on Poetry
Barber for a Week
Sioux Falls Fire Fighter
Christians Are Better Lovers
Beginning Bridge
Filmmaking
Political Activism: Dem. Party
Political Activism: G.O.P.
Kick the Habit, Quit Smoking
Geneology: Climbing Your
  Family Tree
Basics of Hi Fidelity
Teacher Aide
Air National Guard
Workshop for Yearbook
Zoning
Baton Twirling
Band Tour
Needle Point
Varsity Track
Water Color Painting
Bottle Cutting
Women in Literature
How About Flying
Sanitation
Volleyball
Beginning Volleyball
Advanced Bridge
Seed Mosaics
Photography
'Math Brush-Up' Through
  Games
Making Rock Jewelry
Lost Wax Jewelry Making
Individual Learning Experience
Student-for-a-Week at Sioux
  Falls College

Voice Class
Theater Practicum
War Games
Business and Industrial Tours
Furniture Refinishing
String Art
Buying: New and Used
Basketry
Rap with Senior Citizens
Portugese
Karate
Jet Simulation
Macrame
Fun with Frosting
Appreciation of Local History
Super-Graphics
Stamp Collecting
Microbiology
Photography
Vaudeville!!
Nursing
Girls Varsity Track
Silver Smithing
Tour of K-Mart
Wedding Planning
Water Games
Beginning Tennis
Selling Car
Intro to Radio Broadcasting
YMCA: Community Organiza-
  tion
$$$ Money, Money $$$
The Issue Is Life
Advanced Ceramics
Creative Candle Making
Bethany Home for the Aged
A Look at the Stock Market

Appendix C
Abridged List of Minicourses Offered at Keith Valley Middle School, Hatboro-Horsham School District, Pennsylvania

Bird and Plant Identification
Small Engines
TV Workshop
Word Games
Softball Intramurals
Dance Studio
Softball
Soccer
Puzzles/Cryptograms/Secret Codes
Neighborhood Games
Independent Marine Research
School Newspaper
Weight Lifting
Stage Band
Tournament Chess
Chapter 8 or Bust (Allegra)
Remedial Math
Audiovisual Club
Hearts and Pinochle
Photography
Islands of Green (Campus Beautification)
Select Chorus
Independent Marine Study
Decoration Committee
Surveying
Advanced Drawing
Tennis

Gaming Anyone?
Reading for Elementary Schools
Creative Writing
Macrame
Easy Millions
Graphic Arts
Cooking Cool
Photography
Needlepoint
Cartooning
Free Swim and Water Polo
Typing Service
Campers Anonymous
Mixed Chorus
Basketball
Remedial Spanish
Remedial French
Science Help
Introduction to Cooking
Creative Handicrafts
Remedial German
Remedial English and Social Studies
Politics 76
Needlecraft
Model Building
Old Time Radio
Band
Card Games and Tricks

Appendix D
List of Minicourses in English and Social Studies at Jersey Shore High School, Jersey Shore, Pennsylvania

English
Library and Language Skills
American Folklore
The Awakening Years
Mythology
Usage Update
Semantics
School Newspaper
Business Communication I
Business Communication II
Research Paper
The Shadow of Evil
   (Somebody down there
   doesn't like me)
American Songbag
Action and Suspense
So You Want to Be a . . .
Thanatology
The Family
Drugs: Myth and Reality
Shakespeare
The Romantic Viewpoint
The Noble Savage
Future Worlds
Composition I
Composition II
Creative Writing
Social Studies
U.S. History
U.S. Economic History
Introduction to Anthropology
Comparative Religion
Cultural and Urban Geography
U.S. Military History
Immigration and the History of
   Minority Groups
Civil War and Reconstruction

Modern China
The Constitution and
   Bill of Rights
Comparative Government
Party Politics and Voting
Psychology I
Psychology II
Criminology
Social Problems of Jersey Shore
Market Economy
Current Economics Problems
Introduction to Europe
Ancient and Medieval History
Studies in African Cultures
Studies in Latin American
   Cultures
Studies in Far Eastern Cultures
Studies in Middle Eastern
   Cultures
Current History of Russia
Black History of the United
   States
Recent History of the United
   States
Frontier History
American Foreign Pc   ince
   1950
Rise of Western Dictatorships
Contemporary World Problems
Introduction to Sociology
Comparative Economic Systems
Macroeconomics
American Public Finance
International Trade and
   Finance
Geography
U.S. and Canadian Geography

Appendix E
Abridged List of Courses Offered at New Trier East High School, Winnetka, Illinois

Small Farm Planning
Oriental Painting
Ceramics
Rug Making
Silk Screening
Wood Carving
Advertising
Insurance
Gourmet Cooking for Boys
Jazz Dance
Vegetarianism
1950's Films
Tracing Family Trees
History of the Comic Book
Life in England
Indians of the American West
War Games
Stamps
Tropical Fish
Sign Language
Corporate Law
Creative Writing
Acupuncture
First Aid
Kurt Vonnegut
Computer Circuits
Space Travel
Slide Rule Use
Auto Mechanics for Girls
Oceanography
Love
Transactional Analysis
Photography (Beginning)

Transcendental Meditation
Preschool Child
Gestalt Theory
Water Ballet
Dog Training Demonstration
Cinematography
Freudian Psychology
Cave Art
Origami
Lapidary
Astronomy
Ballooning
Human Sexuality
Weight Watching
People Watching
Alternative Schools
Paramedicine
Surgery
Astrology
Body Language
UFO's
Palmistry
ESP
Witchcraft
The Beatles
Energy Crisis
Marriage and Family Life
Bicycle Touring
Golf
Who is Jesus Christ?
Football Scouting
Tennis
Yoga

Kung Fu
Cheerleading
Badminton
Ping-Pong
Rock and Roll
Guitar (beginning)
Tarot Cards

Judo
Horseback
Survival Camping
Animals' Behaviors
Poet Craft Workshop
Child Development

Appendix F
Abridged List of Minicourses at Roosevelt Junior High School, Eugene, Oregon

Advanced Decorative
  Needlework
Baking Magic
American Heritage Cooking
Cartooning and You
Advanced Science Fiction
Cookies and Kids
Debate
Drama I
Chorus I
Foreign Foods
History and Development of
  Writing
Geometry
Homemaking Know-How
Economics in Today's World
World Geography
Ceramics and Sculpture
Basketweaving
Reading Clinic
Field Ecology
Play Reading
Pore Speller 2
Bowling
Percent
Shakespeare I
Cytology: The Biology of Cells
Ecology
Oceanography
American West
Sports History

Bachelor Skills
Do-It-Yourself Room
  Improvement
Drafting
Fly Tying Clinic
Advanced Storytelling
Approaches to Reading
  Literature
Potluck
Machine Woodworking
Sew for Spring
3-D Pictures I
Shutterbug Photography
Music Theater Workshop
Occupations for the 1980's
Creative Photography
Mini-Spanish
Filmmaking
Creative Writing
Grammar for Reading and
  Writing
Folk Ballads
Introduction to Writing
Printmaking Survey
Writing Step by Step
Archery
Occupational Skills
Pre-Algebra
Jogging
Water Sports
World Religions